INTRODUCING
ISSUES WITH
OPPOSING
VIEWPOINTS®

Data Mining

M. M. Eboch, Book Editor

GREENHAVEN
PUBLISHING

Published in 2018 by Greenhaven Publishing, LLC
353 3rd Avenue, Suite 255, New York, NY 10010

Cataloging-in-Publishing Data

Names: Eboch, M.M., editor.
Title: Data mining / edited by M.M. Eboch.
Description: New York : Greenhaven Publishing, 2018. | Series: Introducing issues with opposing viewpoints | Includes bibliographical references and index. | Audience: Grades 9-12.
Identifiers: LCCN ISBN 9781534501966 (library bound) | ISBN 9781534502772 (pbk.)
Subjects: LCSH: Data mining--Juvenile literature.
Classification: LCC QA76.9.D343 D353 2018 | DDC 006.3/12--dc23

Manufactured in the United States of America

Website: http://greenhavenpublishing.com

Contents

Foreword

Indulging in a wide spectrum of ideas, beliefs, and perspectives is a critical cornerstone of democracy. After all, it is often debates over differences of opinion, such as whether to legalize abortion, how to treat prisoners, or when to enact the death penalty, that shape our society and drive it forward. Such diversity of thought is frequently regarded as the hallmark of a healthy and civilized culture. As the Reverend Clifford Schutjer of the First Congregational Church in Mansfield, Ohio, declared in a 2001 sermon, "Surrounding oneself with only like-minded people, restricting what we listen to or read only to what we find agreeable is irresponsible. Refusing to entertain doubts once we make up our minds is a subtle but deadly form of arrogance." With this advice in mind, Introducing Issues with Opposing Viewpoints books aim to open readers' minds to the critically divergent views that comprise our world's most important debates.

Introducing Issues with Opposing Viewpoints simplifies for students the enormous and often overwhelming mass of material now available via print and electronic media. Collected in every volume is an array of opinions that captures the essence of a particular controversy or topic. Introducing Issues with Opposing Viewpoints books embody the spirit of nineteenth-century journalist Charles A. Dana's axiom: "Fight for your opinions, but do not believe that they contain the whole truth, or the only truth." Absorbing such contrasting opinions teaches students to analyze the strength of an argument and compare it to its opposition. From this process readers can inform and strengthen their own opinions, or be exposed to new information that will change their minds. Introducing Issues with Opposing Viewpoints is a mosaic of different voices. The authors are statesmen, pundits, academics, journalists, corporations, and ordinary people who have felt compelled to share their experiences and ideas in a public forum. Their words have been collected from newspapers, journals, books, speeches, interviews, and the Internet, the fastest growing body of opinionated material in the world.

Introducing Issues with Opposing Viewpoints shares many of the well-known features of its critically acclaimed parent series, Opposing

Viewpoints. The articles allow readers to absorb and compare divergent perspectives. Active reading questions preface each viewpoint, requiring the student to approach the material thoughtfully and carefully. Photographs, charts, and graphs supplement each article. A thorough introduction provides readers with crucial background on an issue. An annotated bibliography points the reader toward articles, books, and websites that contain additional information on the topic. An appendix of organizations to contact contains a wide variety of charities, nonprofit organizations, political groups, and private enterprises that each hold a position on the issue at hand. Finally, a comprehensive index allows readers to locate content quickly and efficiently.

Introducing Issues with Opposing Viewpoints is also significantly different from Opposing Viewpoints. As the series title implies, its presentation will help introduce students to the concept of opposing viewpoints and learn to use this material to aid in critical writing and debate. The series' four-color, accessible format makes the books attractive and inviting to readers of all levels. In addition, each viewpoint has been carefully edited to maximize a reader's understanding of the content. Short but thorough viewpoints capture the essence of an argument. A substantial, thought-provoking essay question placed at the end of each viewpoint asks the student to further investigate the issues raised in the viewpoint, compare and contrast two authors' arguments, or consider how one might go about forming an opinion on the topic at hand. Each viewpoint contains sidebars that include at-a-glance information and handy statistics. A Facts About section located in the back of the book further supplies students with relevant facts and figures.

Following in the tradition of the Opposing Viewpoints series, Greenhaven Publishing continues to provide readers with invaluable exposure to the controversial issues that shape our world. As John Stuart Mill once wrote: "The only way in which a human being can make some approach to knowing the whole of a subject is by hearing what can be said about it by persons of every variety of opinion and studying all modes in which it can be looked at by every character of mind. No wise man ever acquired his wisdom in any mode but this." It is to this principle that Introducing Issues with Opposing Viewpoints books are dedicated.

Introduction

"The power of new technologies means that there are fewer and fewer technical constraints on what we can do. That places a special obligation on us to ask tough questions about what we should do."

—President Barack Obama, in a January 17, 2014, address at the Justice Department in Washington, DC.

Data" is a term for facts or statistics collected together. Data mining is the process of examining large sets of data with computers. This process can be used to understand society and analyze trends. Today billions of pieces of data are tracked daily. Computer programs analyze data to see current trends and predict the future. Cities use data to control traffic flow. The government uses data to hunt terrorism. Marketers use data to lure in customers. Scientists use data to predict outbreaks of disease. Data is everywhere, and its use is growing. Yet data collection creates concerns over privacy and security.

The practice of collecting information is not new. Throughout most of human history, records had to be written down and copied by hand. The printing press allowed easier distribution of information in books. More recently, computers caused a data revolution. As computers grew in number and power, massive amounts of data could be collected and stored more easily. Today the Internet allows people to exchange data easily, in seconds. This has created the age of "big data": very large sets of data. A human could not process all that information. But software allows companies and organizations to collect, analyze, and use big data in a variety of ways.

Today big data affects many aspects of society, including business, government, and personal life. People generally do not realize how much data is collected about them. Most people send texts and emails, make phone calls, and search the internet on a regular basis. Often people assume these activities are private. In reality, most online activity can be tracked, from internet searches to social media posts. Mapping software in mobile devices can track the user's location. Credit card, debit, and PayPal transactions are recorded. Software tools can scan the contents of blog posts and online reviews.

Both governments and private companies collect and study data. The government monitors online and phone activity in the name of security. One secret program allowed the US National Security Agency (NSA) to collect information from companies such as Google, Microsoft, Apple, Yahoo, and Facebook. NSA officials could look at a user's search history. They could also access the contents of emails, photos, videos, file transfers, and live chats. In one month in 2013, the NSA collected three billion pieces of data from networks based in the United States. An additional ninety-four billion pieces of data were collected from computer networks worldwide. The NSA gathered information on people's location, contacts, and finances. Most of the information came from people who were not suspected of any crimes. Much of this monitoring is secret, although government agencies are supposed to follow rules to protect privacy.

Advocates of government monitoring claim it can help prevent crime and terrorism. Critics say that government spying violates citizens' privacy rights. Questions also exist about the success of monitoring programs. Some experts claim that less invasive measures would be equally or more successful. The general public is divided on the issue. In a 2014 survey, 40 percent of adults said they disapproved of the government collection of internet and telephone data. Thirty-two percent of respondents approved, while 26 percent reported they were not sure.

Private companies have a different interest in data. Some companies use data to streamline their businesses. Monitoring and understanding data can help a company predict what products will sell so they can keep that stock on hand. Computer programs can analyze the best routes for delivery vehicles, providing faster, more efficient delivery. A company that uses big data properly can save money and keep customers happier.

Companies also use customer data for marketing. Knowing who is most likely to buy a product lets a company target ads at those customers. A company may track what products someone viewed online and then send ads for those products. Data can also help a company improve its customers' experience. A website might predict what someone will want to see based on past behavior. A company might suggest movies, TV shows, or products of interest based on a user's profile.

Marketers often get this data from companies called data brokers. Thousands of data brokers throughout the world specialize in collecting data. One large company, Acxiom, claims to have data on almost every consumer in the United States.

In nearly every aspect of life, big data provides both benefits and challenges. Privacy has become a major concern. Most people do not want complete and absolute privacy. Social media users may give up privacy in order to find online connections. Shoppers may give up privacy in exchange for convenience. For example, an online store that remembers what you ordered in the past makes it easier to order those products again.

Still, most people want more control over who sees their personal information. A 2014 survey from Pew Research Center asked people how they felt about online privacy. 74 percent of respondents felt it was very important to be "in control of who can get information about you." Surveys show that many Americans have concerns about keeping their data private. However, opinions differ on how much privacy people should be willing to give up in exchange for the benefits big data provides.

The next few years may determine how society balances big data and privacy. The answers will affect everyone who uses computers, cell phones, and similar devices. The current debates about big data versus privacy rights are explored in *Introducing Issues with Opposing Viewpoints: Data Mining*, shedding light on this contemporary issue. Contributors offer their diverse perspectives on the impacts of data mining, whether it actually improves society, and how it affects our safety.

Chapter 1

How Does Data Mining Affect the Individual?

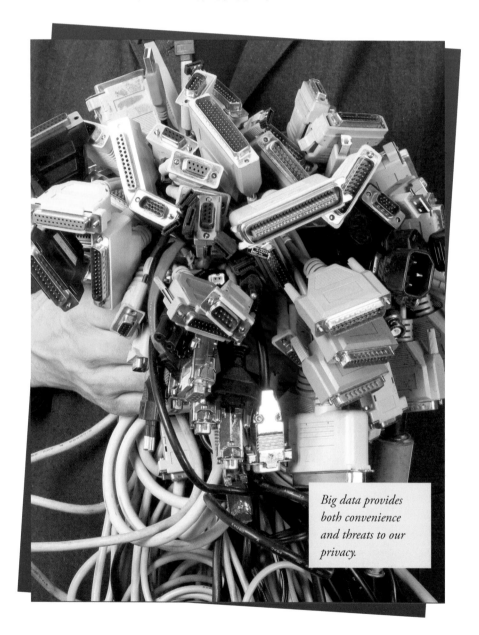

Big data provides both convenience and threats to our privacy.

Viewpoint

1

Data Brokers Know All About You

Lois Beckett

"Is it necessary for someone to track that I recently bought underwear online?"

In the following viewpoint, Lois Beckett explores the world of data brokers. More than two hundred data broker companies collect all kinds of information on people. This includes consumer data (what you buy) and social media activity. Companies can connect this data with demographic information, such as race and age. Often this data is used for marketing, targeting people with ads. Yet the information is not always correct. Most people have no idea how much information is collected. Legally, consumers do not have a right to view the data collected about them. Some companies allow people to "opt out" of data collection. Yet the process is often difficult and time-consuming. Some government agencies are pushing for new privacy rules. Marketers argue that stricter rules are not necessary. Beckett is a ProPublica reporter covering politics, big data, and information privacy issues.

We've spent a lot of time this past year trying to understand how the National Security Agency gathers and stores information about ordinary people. But there's also a thriving public market for data on individual Americans—especially data about the things we buy and might want to buy.

Consumer data companies are scooping up huge amounts of consumer information about people around the world and selling it, providing marketers details about whether you're pregnant or divorced or trying to lose weight, about how rich you are and what kinds of cars you drive. But many people still don't know data brokers exist.

The Federal Trade Commission is pushing the companies to give consumers more information and control over what happens to their data. The White House released a report this May outlining concerns that these detailed consumer profiles might lead to race or income-based discrimination—what the White House called "digital redlining."

It's very hard to tell who is collecting or sharing your data—or what kinds of information companies are collecting. Early this year, Office Max sent a letter to a grieving father addressed to his name, followed by "daughter killed in car crash."

Here's a look at what we know—and what we don't—about the consumer data industry.

How Much Do These Companies Know About Individual People?

They start with the basics, like names, addresses and contact information, and add on demographics, like age, race, occupation and "edu-

Stores often sell information about their customers to consumer data companies. Customer loyalty programs can provide savings benefits, but are they worth the loss of privacy?

cation level," according to consumer data firm Acxiom's overview of its various categories.

But that's just the beginning: The companies collect lists of people experiencing "life-event triggers" like getting married, buying a home, sending a kid to college—or even getting divorced.

Credit reporting giant Experian has a separate marketing services division, which sells lists of "names of expectant parents and families with newborns" that are "updated weekly."

The companies also collect data about your hobbies and many of the purchases you make. Want to buy a list of people who read romance novels? Epsilon can sell you that, as well as a list of people who donate to international aid charities.

A subsidiary of credit reporting company Equifax even collects detailed salary and pay stub information for roughly 38 percent of employed Americans, as NBC news reported. As part of handling employee verification requests, the company gets the information directly from employers.

Equifax said in a statement that the information is only sold to customers "who have been verified through a detailed credentialing process." It added that if a mortgage company or other lender wants to access information about your salary, they must obtain your permission to do so.

Of course, data companies typically don't have all of this information on any one person. As Acxiom notes in its overview, "No individual record ever contains all the possible data." And some of the data these companies sell is really just a guess about your background or preferences, based on the characteristics of your neighborhood, or other people in a similar age or demographic group.

Where Are They Getting All This Info?

The stores where you shop sell it to them.

Datalogix, for instance, which collects information from store loyalty cards, says it has information on more than $1 trillion in consumer spending "across 1400+ leading brands." It doesn't say which ones. (Datalogix did not respond to our requests for comment.)

Data companies usually refuse to say exactly what companies sell them information, citing competitive reasons. And retailers also don't make it easy for you to find out whether they're selling your information.

But thanks to California's "Shine the Light" law, researchers at U.C. Berkeley were able to get a small glimpse of how companies sell or share your data. The study recruited volunteers to ask more than 80 companies how the volunteers' information was being shared.

Only two companies actually responded with details about how volunteers' information had been shared. Upscale furniture store Restoration Hardware said that it had sent "your name, address and what you purchased" to seven other companies, including a data "cooperative" that allows retailers to pool data about customer transactions, and another company that later became part of Datalogix. (Restoration Hardware hasn't responded to our request for comment.)

Walt Disney also responded and described sharing even more information: not just a person's name and address and what they purchased, but their age, occupation, and the number, age and gender of their children. It listed companies that received data, among them companies owned by Disney, like ABC and ESPN, as well as others, including Honda, HarperCollins Publishing, Almay cosmetics, and yogurt company Dannon.

But Disney spokeswoman Zenia Mucha said that Disney's letter, sent in 2007, "wasn't clear" about how the data was actually shared with different companies on the list. Outside companies like Honda only received personal information as part of a contest, sweepstakes, or other joint promotion that they had done with Disney, Mucha said. The data was shared "for the fulfillment of that contest prize, not for their own marketing purposes."

Where Else Do Data Brokers Get Information About Me?

Government records and other publicly available information, including some sources that may surprise you. Your state Department of Motor Vehicles, for instance, may sell personal information— like your name, address, and the type of vehicles you own—to data companies, although only for certain permitted purposes, including identify verification.

Public voting records, which include information about your party registration and how often you vote, can also be bought and sold for commercial purposes in some states.

Are There Limits to the Kinds of Data These Companies Can Buy and Sell?

Yes, certain kinds of sensitive data are protected—but much of your information can be bought and sold without any input from you.

Federal law protects the confidentiality of your medical records and your conversations with your doctor. There are also strict rules regarding the sale of information used to determine your credit-worthiness, or your eligibility for employment, insurance and housing. For instance, consumers have the right to view and correct their own credit reports, and potential employers have to ask for your consent before they buy a credit report about you.

Other than certain kinds of protected data—including medical records and data used for credit reports—consumers have no legal right to control or even monitor how information about them is bought and sold. As the FTC notes, "There are no current laws requiring data brokers to maintain the privacy of consumer data unless they use that data for credit, employment, insurance, housing, or other similar purposes."

So They Don't Sell Information About My Health?

Actually, they do.

Data companies can capture information about your "interests" in certain health conditions based on what you buy—or what you search for online. Datalogix has lists of people classified as "allergy sufferers" and "dieters." Acxiom sells data on whether an individual has an "online search propensity" for a certain "ailment or prescription."

Consumer data is also beginning to be used to evaluate whether you're making healthy choices.

One health insurance company recently bought data on more than three million people's consumer purchases in order to flag health-related actions, like purchasing plus-sized clothing, the Wall Street Journal reported. (The company bought purchasing information for current plan members, not as part of screening people for potential coverage.)

Spokeswoman Michelle Douglas said that Blue Cross and Blue Shield of North Carolina would use the data to target free programming offers to their customers.

Douglas suggested that it might be more valuable for companies to use consumer data "to determine ways to help me improve my health" rather than "to buy my data to send me pre-paid credit card applications or catalogs full of stuff they want me to buy."

Do Companies Collect Information About My Social Media Profiles and What I Do Online?

Yes.

As we highlighted last year, some data companies record—and then resell—all kinds of information you post online, including your screen names, website addresses, interests, hometown and professional history, and how many friends or followers you have.

Acxiom said it collects information about which social media sites individual people use, and "whether they are a heavy or a light user," but that they do not collect information about "individual postings" or your "lists of friends."

More traditional consumer data can also be connected with information about what you do online. Datalogix, the company that collects loyalty card data, has partnered with Facebook to track whether Facebook users who see ads for certain products actually end up buying them at local stores, as the Financial Times reported in 2012.

In fact, the effort to connect online and offline information about you is one of the hottest new trends in the data industry. Companies are increasingly trying to use information about your offline purchases to target you online.

And it's not limited to what you buy: in the 2012 elections, companies were able to match your voting record to a cookie on your computer—allowing candidates to target you with online ads based on whether you're a registered Democrat or Republican—or how much you donated to political campaigns before.

Is There a Way to Find Out Exactly What These Data Companies Know About Me?

Not really—although that's beginning to change.

You have the right to review and correct your credit report. But with marketing data, there's often no way to know exactly what information is attached to your name—or whether it's accurate.

Most companies offer, at best, a partial picture.

ProPublica's Julia Angwin requested information about herself from data brokers, and was "equally irked by the reports that were wrong—data brokers who thought I was a single mother with no education—as I was by the ones that were correct—is it necessary for someone to track that I recently bought underwear online?"

In September 2013, Acxiom debuted aboutthedata.com, which allows to you review and edit some of the company's marketing data on you, by entering your name, address, birth date and the last four digits of your social security number.

The Federal Trade Commission's Julie Brill tweeted that "more data brokers should follow" Acxiom's example. But the effort received mixed reviews from users, privacy advocates and government regulators, the New York Times reported.

Previously, Acxiom only let customers review a smaller slice of the information the company sells about them, including criminal history, as New York Times reporter Natasha Singer described in 2012. When Singer requested and finally received her report in 2012, all it included was a record of her residential addresses.

Other companies also offer some access. A spokeswoman for Epsilon said it allows consumers to review "high level information" about their data—like whether or not you've purchased "home furnishings" merchandise. (Requests to review this information cost $5 and can only be made by postal mail.)

RapLeaf, a company that advertises that it has "real-time data" on 80 percent of U.S. email addresses, says it gives customers "total control over the data we have on you," and allows them to review and edit the categories it associates with them (like "estimated household income" and "Likely Political Contributor to Republicans").

How Do I Know When Someone Has Purchased Data About Me?

Most of the time, you don't.

When you're checking out at a store and a cashier asks you for your Zip code, the store isn't just getting that single piece of information. Acxiom and other data companies offer services that allow stores to use your Zip code and the name on your credit card to pinpoint your home address— without asking you for it directly.

Is There Any Way to Stop the Companies from Collecting and Sharing Information About Me?

Sometimes—but it requires a whole lot of work.

Some data brokers offer consumers the chance to "opt out" of being included in their databases, or at least from receiving advertising enabled by that company. Rapleaf, for instance, has a "Permanent opt-out" that "deletes information associated with your email address from the Rapleaf database."

But to actually opt-out effectively, you need to know about all the different data brokers and where to find their opt-outs. Most consumers, of course, don't have that information.

We collected a list of data brokers that will give you copies of your data, and another list of data brokers that allow you to opt-out.

Of the 212 data brokers she identified, less than half—92—accepted opt-outs. For most of them, the opt-out process was laborious. Many required her to submit some form of identification, such as a driver's license, in order to opt out. In some cases, she wrote, "I decided not to opt-out because the service seemed so sketchy that I didn't want to send in any additional information."

But she was able to clear her information from some databases: "A search for my name on some of the largest people-search websites, such as Intelius and Spokeo, yields no relevant results," she wrote.

In a 2012 privacy report, the FTC suggested that data brokers should create a centralized website that would make it easier for consumers to learn about the existence of these companies and their rights regarding the data they collect.

How Many People Do These Companies Have Information On?

Basically everyone in the U.S. and many beyond it. Acxiom, recently profiled by the New York Times, says it has information on 500 million people worldwide, including "nearly every U.S. consumer."

After the 9/11 attacks, CNN reported, Acxiom was able to locate 11 of the 19 hijackers in its database.

How Is All of This Data Actually Used?

Mostly to sell you stuff. Companies want to buy lists of people who might be interested in what they're selling—and also want to learn more about their current customers.

They also sell their information for other purposes, including identity verification, fraud prevention and background checks.

If New Privacy Laws Are Passed, Will They Include the Right to See What Data These Companies Have Collected About Me?

Unlikely.

In a 2012 report on privacy, the Federal Trade Commission recommended that Congress pass legislation "that would provide consumers with access to information about them held by a data broker." President Barack Obama has also proposed a Consumer Privacy Bill of Rights that would give consumers the right to access and correct certain information about them.

But this probably won't include access to marketing data, which the Federal Trade Commission considers less sensitive than data used for credit reports or identity verification.

In terms of marketing data, "we think at the very least consumers should have access to the general categories of data the companies have about consumers," said Maneesha Mithal of the FTC's Division of Privacy and Identity Protection.

Data companies have also pushed back against the idea of opening up marketing profiles for individual consumers' inspection.

Even if there were errors in your marketing data profile, "the worst thing that could happen is that you get an advertising offer that isn't relevant to you," said Rachel Thomas, the vice president of government affairs at the Direct Marketing Association.

"The fraud and security risks that you run by opening up those files is higher than any potential harm that could happen to the consumer," Thomas said.

EVALUATING THE AUTHOR'S ARGUMENTS:

In this viewpoint Lois Beckett quotes people who do not like the amount of information data brokers collect. Marketers claim this information is harmless and may even benefit people. Could it hurt someone to have companies know about their purchases and online activity?

Big Data Has the Potential to Discriminate

Jason Furman and Tim Simcoe

"Discriminatory pricing can pose difficult trade-offs and present serious concerns about fairness."

In the following viewpoint Jason Furman and Tim Simcoe describe a study involving big data, as part of an Obama administration initiative on big data and privacy. The study looked at companies that charge different prices to different people, a practice known as "differential pricing." Overall, differential pricing can benefit consumers (like giving discounts to seniors) as well as businesses. However, it also could be used to unfairly discriminate against some customers. The White House study group suggested that consumers should have more control over what information companies can collect. Furman was an economic adviser to President Obama. Simcoe was a senior economist for that council.

AS YOU READ, CONSIDER THE FOLLOWING QUESTIONS:

1. How can differential pricing benefit consumers, according to the viewpoint?
2. According to the authors, how many different ways are companies experimenting with pricing strategies?
3. How might big data help prevent discrimination in pricing, according to the viewpoint?

"The Economics of Big Data and Differential Pricing," by Jason Furman and Tim Simcoe, USA.gov, February 6, 2015.

This morning, the White House released an update to the big data working group's May 2014 report on big data, describing progress in implementing the working group's recommendations throughout the government. As part of that process, the Council of Economic Advisers released a new study on big data and differential pricing.

Differential pricing is the practice of charging different prices to different customers. Economic textbooks typically refer to this as "price discrimination." Everyday examples include discounts for senior citizens at the movie-theater and higher priced tickets for last minute business travelers.

Economists have studied differential pricing for many years, and while big data seems poised to revolutionize pricing in practice, it has not altered the underlying principles. Perhaps surprisingly, those principles suggest that differential pricing is often good for both firms and their customers. When prices reflect a buyer's ability to pay, sellers can often serve customers who would otherwise get priced out of the market, as with need-based financial aid for college students. Price differences can also reflect the cost or risk of serving different customers, which can discourage inappropriate risk-taking and expand the size of the market.

Concerns About Fairness

The benefits of differential pricing indicate that it can play an important positive role in the overall economy. However, our report also explains how discriminatory pricing can pose difficult trade-offs and present serious concerns about fairness, especially when consumers are unaware of how sellers are using information about them, or when pricing is based on factors outside of individuals' control. One way to limit to unfair or inaccurate applications of big data in this context is to give consumers increased visibility into the types of information that companies collect, and more control over how it is used, as proposed in the President's Consumer Privacy Bill of Rights.

Big data allows companies to collect more information about customers and use it to create new kinds of measures, raising the likelihood differential pricing will become more common and more personalized over time. Our review of differential pricing online re-

The information you post on social media can be collected as data, unbeknownst to you.

vealed that companies are presently experimenting with three broad pricing strategies: (1) experiments that randomly manipulate prices to learn about demand; (2) efforts to steer consumers towards particular products without altering their prices; and (3) using big data to customize prices to individual buyers. Research on the prevalence of these pricing practices suggests that experiments and steering are common at some web sites, while cases of personalized pricing remain limited. Nevertheless, there is some evidence that personalized pricing could prove very profitable, providing strong incentives for companies to continue experimenting with these tools.

Helping the Consumer

Our report also finds evidence that big data and related technologies can empower individual buyers. In the online environment, for ex-

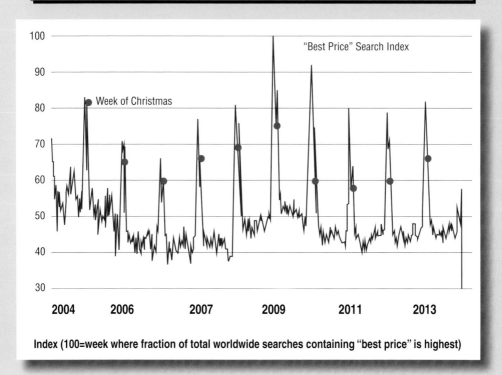

Google Searches for "Best Price"

"Best Price" Search Index

Week of Christmas

Index (100=week where fraction of total worldwide searches containing "best price" is highest)

Source: Google Trends

ample, many Internet browsers have privacy settings that allow users to control their personal information. Buyers can also use tools like price tracking and comparison web sites, or even a simple search engine, to seek out the best available price. For example, the chart above shows the relative frequency of Google searches on the term "best price" and how it is strongly correlated with the holiday shopping season. Partly because of these tools, and the competition they foster, Americans are using the Internet to shop in rapidly growing numbers.

Differential pricing in high-stakes transactions such as employment, insurance or credit provision can raise substantial concerns regarding privacy, data quality and fairness. In these settings, big data may facilitate discriminatory pricing strategies that target consumers based on factors outside their own control, or run afoul of antidiscrimination provisions in existing laws such as the Fair Credit Reporting Act or Civil Rights Act. Here too, however, big data can be a tool that works for consumers. For example, where the law protects specific groups against discriminatory pricing, big data can be used to conduct audits for disparate impact that help detect problems, both before and perhaps after a discriminatory algorithm is used on real consumers.

Given the speed at which both the technology and business practices are evolving, the CEA report on Big Data and Differential Pricing provides only a first look at a set of issues that will keep economists, engineers and policy makers busy for many years. The long-run challenge in this area is to promote the use of big data and differential pricing where they help to expand markets, while preventing unfair discrimination based on sensitive information that consumers may not understand they have revealed.

EVALUATING THE AUTHOR'S ARGUMENTS:

In this viewpoint, Jason Furman and Tim Simcoe claim that differential pricing has many benefits. However, they also warn against potential problems. How might allowing consumers to have control of their information help prevent problems?

Data Surveillance Is All Around Us, and It Will Change Our Behavior

Uri Gal

"How many of us know who can see our Facebook likes, Google searches, or Uber rides, and what they use these data for?"

In the following viewpoint Uri Gal offers warnings about the collection and use of data. He notes that companies monitor our computers and mobile devices. Wearable technology allows bodies to be monitored as well. This means that companies may know almost everything a person does. Marketers can tell if someone visited a store after seeing an ad. Companies may know when and how someone exercises and even how well the person sleeps. Predictive analytics goes a step further. It uses past behavior to predict future behavior. Companies and even the government may then try to affect behavior. Rewards may be offered for "good" behavior and punishments for "bad" behavior. Gal is an associate professor in business information systems at the University of Sydney.

AS YOU READ, CONSIDER THE FOLLOWING QUESTIONS:
1. How do electronic devices allow companies to monitor people's behavior?
2. What kind of information could a company get from a health app?
3. How can companies use data to reward people for good behavior or punish people for bad behavior?

Enabled by exponential technological advancements in data storage, transmission and analysis, the drive to "datify" our lives is creating an ultra-transparent world where we are never free from being under surveillance.

Increasing aspects of our lives are now recorded as digital data that are systematically stored, aggregated, analysed, and sold. Despite the promise of big data to improve our lives, all encompassing data surveillance constitutes a new form of power that poses a risk not only to our privacy, but to our free will.

Data surveillance started out with online behaviour tracking designed to help marketers customise their messages and offerings. Driven by companies aiming to provide personalised product, service and content recommendations, data were utilised to generate value for customers.

But data surveillance has become increasingly invasive and its scope has broadened with the proliferation of the internet-of-things and embedded computing. The former expands surveillance to our homes, cars, and daily activities by harvesting data from smart and mobile devices. The latter extends surveillance and places it inside our bodies where biometric data can be collected.

Two characteristics of data surveillance enable its expansion.

It's Multifaceted

Data are used to track and circumscribe people's behaviour across space and time dimensions. An example of space-based tracking is geo-marketing. With access to real-time physical location data, marketers can send tailored ads to consumers' mobile devices to prompt

Wearable technology, such as smart watches and activity trackers, makes it even easier for companies to track users and in turn manipulate their behavior.

them to visit stores in their vicinity. To maximise their effectiveness, marketers can tailor the content and timing of ads based on consumers' past and current location behaviours, sometimes without consumers' consent.

Location data from GPS or street maps can only approximate a person's location. But with recent technology, marketers can accurately determine whether a consumer has been inside a store or merely passed by it. This way they can check whether serving ads has resulted in a store visit, and refine subsequent ads.

Health applications track and structure people's time. They allow users to plan daily activities, schedule workouts, and monitor their progress. Some applications enable users to plan their caloric intake over time. Other applications let users track their sleep pattern.

While users can set their initial health goals, many applications rely on the initial information to structure a progress plan that includes recommended rest times, workout load, caloric intake, and sleep. Applications can send users notifications to ensure compliance with the plan: a reminder that a workout is overdue; a warning that a caloric limit is reached; or a positive reinforcement when a goal has been reached. Despite the sensitive nature of these data, it is not uncommon that they are sold to third parties.

It's Opaque and Distributed

Our digital traces are collected by multiple governmental and business entities which engage in data exchange through markets whose structure is mostly hidden from people.

Data are typically classified into three categories: first-party, which companies gather directly from their customers through their website, app, or customer-relationship-management system; second-party, which is another company's first-party data and is acquired directly from it, and; third-party, which is collected, aggregated, and sold by specialised data vendors.

Despite the size of this market, how data are exchanged through it remains unknown to most people (how many of us know who can see our Facebook likes, Google searches, or Uber rides, and what they use these data for?).

Some data surveillance applications go beyond recording to predicting behavioural trends.

Predictive analytics are used in healthcare, public policy, and management to render organisations and people more productive. Growing in popularity, these practices have raised serious ethical concerns around social inequality, social discrimination, and privacy. They have also sparked a debate about what predictive big data can be used for.

It's Nudging Us

A more worrying trend is the use of big data to manipulate human behaviour at scale by incentivising "appropriate" activities, and penalising "inappropriate" activities. In recent years, governments in the UK, US, and Australia have been experimenting with attempts to "correct" the behaviour of their citizens through "nudge units."

With the application of big data, the scope of such efforts can be greatly extended. For instance, based on data acquired (directly or indirectly) from your favourite health app, your insurance company could raise your rates if it determined your lifestyle to be unhealthy. Based on the same data, your bank could classify you as a "high-risk customer" and charge you a higher interest on your loan.

Using data from your smart car, your car insurance company could decrease your premium if it deemed your driving to be safe.

By signalling "appropriate behaviours" companies and governments aim to shape our behaviour. As the scope of data surveillance increases, more of our behaviours will be evaluated and "corrected" and this disciplinary drive will become increasingly inescapable.

With this disciplinary drive becoming routine, there is a danger we will start to accept it as the norm, and pattern our own behaviour to comply with external expectations, to the detriment of our free will.

The "datafication" of our lives is an undeniable trend which is impacting all of us. However, its societal consequences are not predetermined. We need to have an open discussion about its nature and implications, and about the kind of society we want to live in.

EVALUATING THE AUTHOR'S ARGUMENTS:

In this viewpoint Uri Gal notes that big data can be used to encourage or discourage behavior. Both companies and governments may already be manipulating behavior in this way. Is it reasonable to claim that these policies interfere with free will?

Surveillance Can Go Too Far

"Social media is often just about passing along gossip or giving a thumbs up to a joke. But those actions can get a student in trouble."

National Coalition Against Censorship

In the following viewpoint the National Coalition Against Censorship (NCAC) examines some ways in which schools may censor students' social media use. On the one hand, schools have a responsibility to keep students safe. This can mean stopping students from bullying through social media. On the other hand, students have a right to free speech. But schools can—and have—disciplined students for inappropriate social media posts. In some cases, this has led to students suing schools in protest of disciplinary actions. In many court cases, students have won the lawsuits on the grounds of freedom of speech. The NCAC is an alliance of nonprofit groups and is dedicated to opposing censorship in all forms.

AS YOU READ, CONSIDER THE FOLLOWING QUESTIONS:
1. Do students have a legal right to free speech, even at school?
2. When can students legally be punished for speech on or off campus?
3. What kind of speech seems most likely to be punished by schools, according to the examples in this article?

"Watch What You Tweet: Schools, Censorship, and Social Media," National Coalition Against Censorship. Reprinted by permission.

Many high school students can hardly imagine life without Facebook, Twitter, SnapChat, and Instagram. These platforms offer a chance for young people to speak without adult supervision or intervention.

That makes many adults very, very nervous—especially the adults who are in charge of operating public schools.

Of course there are times when it is right to be concerned about what's happening online; administrators and educators are tasked with maintaining a healthy and respectful learning environment free from harassment.

But how lawmakers and school officials police social media can have serious implications for youth free expression. We have seen students punished for online speech that was discovered by faculty, reported by other students or with the aid of surveillance companies like SnapTrends, CompuGuardian, Gaggle, and Social Sentinel Inc. Punishment for speech often comes under the veneer of keeping schools "safe," whether from physical violence or emotional distress.

But how far can that authority legally extend? When do schools go too far in policing student speech online? As we'll explain, the lines are not as clear as one might think.

Student Speech in the Courts

"It can hardly be argued that either students or teachers shed their constitutional rights to freedom of speech or expression at the school-house gate."

The key Supreme Court case on school censorship is *Tinker v. Des Moines Independent Community School District* (1969). A group of students had been suspended for protesting the Vietnam War by wearing black armbands to school. The justices ruled in their favor, establishing one of the guiding principles in the cases that would follow: This case, and others like it, establish the rights of students to speak out so long as their words did not constitute a "material disruption" of a school's educational activities.

That case presented one standard—speech that "materially and substantially disrupts the work and discipline of the school" can be the basis of some punishment or sanction.

Of course, there are bound to be different ideas about what con-

Students should be mindful of their social media presence. While they have a right to free speech, there are limitations.

stitutes a "material disruption." And subsequent court decisions have not always clarified what kinds of speech—either in school newspapers, off-campus publications or any other venues—is permissible or punishable.

In the 1986 case *Bethel v. Fraser*, the Court ruled that a student could be punished for delivering a speech during an assembly that was "offensively lewd and indecent" and thus undermined the school's educational mission. There was not an argument that the speech caused a disruption.

Almost 20 years later, the *Morse v. Frederick* decision offered another case that helped define the contours of students' First Amendment rights. At a school-sanctioned, off-campus event, a student held up a banner that read, "Bong Hits for Jesus." The school's suspension of the student was upheld on the grounds that the student's speech could be "reasonably viewed as promoting illegal drug use," an activity that the school would want to discourage.

Off-Campus Internet Speech

But what are the standards when the speech in question is happening away from school, but might be seen by students or address issues that are happening on campus? In 2007 a Connecticut high school student posted critical comments about school officials after a dispute over a battle of the bands event. In response, school administrators barred the student, Avery Doninger, from student government. She sued, and a district court ruled that the school's punishment was justified on the grounds that her call for readers to complain to the school was disruptive. That ruling was upheld in 2011 by the U.S. Court of Appeals for the Second Circuit.

Other cases have involved students directly mocking school officials. In 2005 high school senior Justin Layshock made a MySpace profile to mock his principal, and was suspended. His parents decided to sue, and they prevailed in a Third Circuit decision, which found no reason to consider the site a material disruption.

A similar case emerged around the same time when a Pennsylvania middle school student created another parody MySpace profile for her principal. The school's suspension was upheld in two court decisions, one of which determined that the school could lawfully punish "vulgar, lewd, and potentially illegal speech that had an effect on campus." In a 2010 appeal to the full Third Circuit, several free speech groups argued that the threshold established in one of those cases was inconsistent with other decisions by the same court. The following year, the court overturned the earlier decision, and found the school's discipline violated the student's First Amendment rights.

Busted: Fifteen Times Students Got in Trouble For Speaking

Whatever a public school or district's policy might be, how they react to real-life cases is where the rubber meets the road. And there are plenty of examples of schools taking extreme measures against students who were engaged in speech that, while perhaps ill-advised, rude, or offensive, was fully protected.

Pot Picture? You're Off the Team

Ohio high school student Jakob Neumann was suspended from the soccer team for retweeting a message about marijuana. His father complained that there was a "constitutional issue" in play: "It happened during the summer vacation, on our home computer—and he didn't make any mention of the school or the team."

The school initially suspended Neumann from the team for an entire year, then reduced the penalty to a third of the season after an appeal was filed. After he says an administrator hassled him at a school function, Neumann decided to file suit.

Suspended Over Anti-Bullying Video

In 2012, a high school freshman decided to make an anti-bullying video for an assignment on persuasive speech. But school officials in Longwood, New York gave her more than a bad grade: they suspended her.

The video was about a fictional character who, among other things, receives taunting and abusive messages on Facebook. A parent at the school didn't know the account portrayed in the video was fake, and she informed school officials, who took action because the video posed a "substantial disruption." But after local media took up the case, the school reversed its decision.

Whistleblowing? You're Out

The same can't be said for a student in Pickerington, Ohio, who re-posted a racially charged video on Twitter to expose the behavior of two of his fellow students. All three were disciplined, with the sophomore whistleblower receiving a 10-day suspension and a threat of expulsion. He was told that because he had re-posted the video during class, it created an "educational disruption." Never mind the fact that he was standing up against something threatening to 25 percent of the student population, just three months after another image of a student wearing a KKK costume circulated on Snapchat.

It Doesn't Matter that You Didn't Write It

Social media is often just about passing along gossip or giving a thumbs up to a joke. But those actions can get a student in trouble. In 2014, South Carolina senior Demi Grant got into trouble for "favoriting" messages on a gossipy feed because she thought they were funny. School officials didn't agree. They reportedly called a few dozen students into the library for a meeting about the Twitter account in question. Many of them were disciplined, but Grant was suspended for five days.

In Salem, Oregon, 20 students at McKay High School were suspended for retweeting a message from a feed called "Salem Confessions" that suggested a teacher flirted with students. The state ACLU called the punishments "a clear violation of both the United States and Oregon Constitutions." After the controversy made headlines, the school would up expunging the students' suspensions.

Hand Over Your Password

In 2012 a twelve-year old Minnesota student wrote that she "hated" a hall monitor at school. Somehow her principal at Minnewaska Area Middle School found out and called her into a meeting to tell her she would receive detention for bullying. When she wrote a follow up on Facebook wondering who told on her, the school suspended her. That wasn't it; after a complaint from a parent later that year, the same student was called into a meeting and told she would have to give school officials her password. The student sued, and won a $70,000 judgment—and the school changed its policies regarding social media.

Jeering New Cheering Rules

In January 2016 the Wisconsin Interscholastic Athletic Association sent out an email laying out new rules concerning behavior at student sporting events. Popular chants like "Air ball!" were now out. And one student athlete decided to have a little fun with the new rules. Hilbert High School's April Gehl, who plays three sports, wrote a three word response: Eat shit WIAA."

Not everyone thought it was funny. The athletic association apparently spoke to school officials, and Gehl was suspended for five games. Gehl didn't challenge the punishment, but had this to say: "I was like, 'Really? For tweeting my opinion?' I thought it was ridiculous."

That Joke Isn't Funny

Two words can get you suspended. Reid Sagehorn was an honors student at Minnesota's Rogers High School, and captain of the football and basketball teams. But that didn't matter to school officials when they found out that he had posted a message on a "Rogers Confessions" twitter page. In response to a question about making out with a teacher, Sagehorn responded—"Actually, yes"—which he insisted was not meant to be taken seriously.

The school suspended him for 5 days, and then increased the penalty to two months. He withdrew from the school, but he and his parents decided to fight the suspension. After a district court ruled that Sagehorn's case could move forward, in December 2015 the district decided to settle for $425,000.

He Blows? You'd Better Apologize

When high school senior Emma Brown visited the Kansas state capitol she apparently got a look at Governor Sam Brownback. She wasn't impressed, posting this message on Twitter: "Just made mean comments at gov. brownback and told him he sucked, in person #heblowsalot." A member of the governor's staff wasn't amused, and contacted the student group that organized the trip to complain. When word got to Sullivan's school, her principal called her into a meeting and demanded that she go into "damage control" mode and write an apology.

To her credit, Sullivan refused—and the governor wound up apologizing. It's good that a student was able to teach a valuable First Amendment lesson to a group of powerful grown ups.

Good for Trump, Bad for You

As part of a homework assignment that involve watching a Republican presidential debate, Revere High School student Caley Godino tweeted something that she thought sounded like candidate Donald Trump. Responding to a teacher's comment about low voter turnout, she wrote that "only 10 percent of Revere votes for mayor cause the other 90 percent isn't legal." Revere superintendent Dianne Kelley insisted to a local TV newscast that the Massachusetts district supports free speech, but they have a funny way of showing it: Godino was removed from the cheerleading team for the rest of the year.

Bullying or Political Disagreement?

New Jersey high school student Bethany Koval was called into the principal's office and given a serious warning: She may have broken the state's anti-bullying law. But her possible "crime" seemed to amount to getting into an argument about Mideast politics.

Another student at Fair Lawn High School was upset by their interaction and went to school officials to complain, leading to her meeting with an assistant principal who warned that "what you put out electronically can also get you in trouble in school. Koval responded by saying that having controversial opinions shouldn't be a problem, he replied, "There's a state law that might interpret it different." Koval recorded the interaction, and the incident received news coverage around the world.

Settlement Over School-Hating Site

In one of the earliest student social media speech controversies, Ryan Dwyer was suspended and temporarily removed from the Maple

Place Middle School baseball team in 2005 for creating an "Anti-Maple Place" website. The site called his New Jersey school "downright boring" and offered a guest book in which visitors could share their own distaste (however, it told them not to curse or threaten teachers). Dwyer took down the private, off-campus site after a week at school officials' request, and filed suit after receiving the aforementioned punishment.

The case was settled in Dwyer's favor to the tune of $117,500, with a district court determining administrators had indeed violated his First Amendment rights.

Profanity at Home
In 2012, Garrett High School in Indianapolis expelled senior Austin Carroll after, late one night at home, he tweeted [a string of profanities]. School officials claimed they were in the right because Carroll had used a school-issued computer or email account to issue the tweet, thus violating students' internet "Respectable Use Policy."

Carroll insisted that he had used his own computer, and the Respectable Use Policy did not specifically mention foul language or students' personal social media posts. The school's action drew widespread attention, and some were especially outraged by the fact that the school seemed to be tracking students' social media posts as a matter of policy. Carroll did not, in the end, challenge the school's actions.

Suspended for... Insulting the Football Team?
In May 2013, the senior class president at Heights High School in Kansas was suspended for a serious infraction: Making fun of the school's hapless football team.

Wesley Teague was suspended for the remainder of the school year after tweeting "'Heights U' is equivalent to WSU's football team." Though seemingly innocuous to an outsider—there is no longer a team at WSU (Wichita State University), school officials claimed the comparison "acted to incite a disturbance" and "aggressively disrespected many athletes."

Teague, a student athlete himself, could no longer give the commencement speech at graduation. He had 'bullied' the football team.

Harsh Hashtag Backlash

There are always debates about how schools should spend their money. But students might not get a vote—or a voice. In June 2013, Cicero-North Syracuse High School senior Pat Brown was suspended for three days after creating the Twitter hashtag "#shitCNSshouldcut," jokingly suggesting ways his New York school could save money in the wake of failed budget changes. The principal accused Brown of harassing him and "inciting a social media riot that disrupted the learning environment."

Preventing Fights or Preventing Scrutiny?

In Huntsville, Alabama, where superintendent Casey Wardynski was under fire in 2014 for surreptitiously monitoring students' social media accounts for 18 months after claiming he received a "tip" from the NSA (proven untrue), one student was expelled in February 2016 for filming a fight on school grounds and then posting it online. Wardynski instituted a new policy stating that it was under the district's authority to prevent fights by monitoring students on social media, and insisted that students who posted the videos were looking for attention.

After the student's family hired a lawyer to contest the expulsion, her punishment was overturned. It's still not clear if such an act would be cause for such extreme measures in the city in the future.

EVALUATING THE AUTHOR'S ARGUMENTS:

In this viewpoint the National Coalition Against Censorship describe cases where students were punished for their words. The coalition suggests that in these cases, the schools wrongly punished students for protected free speech. How can one determine appropriate standards for whether speech is a disruption that should be punished?

Viewpoint 5

Corporate Cybersnooping Is a Big Business

Stephanie Simon and Josh Gerstein

"We cannot even conceive of the ways our data is collected and then used to manipulate us at our weakest moments."

In the following viewpoint Stephanie Simon and Josh Gerstein explore the data collected by private companies and maintain that many people are concerned about the government prying into private life. However, businesses likely have even more data on the average US consumer than the government does. Much of this data collection has positive benefits for consumers. At its best, data helps make lives easier and more comfortable, according to those in favor of it. Yet people give up a great deal of privacy in order to get these benefits. Simon was senior education writer for Politico and is currently managing editor of news for STAT. Gerstein is senior White House reporter for Politico.

AS YOU READ, CONSIDER THE FOLLOWING QUESTIONS:

1. What are some benefits to letting companies collect data about your behavior?
2. What are some risks to letting companies collect that data?
3. What percentage of people who viewed the data collected on them wanted that data destroyed?

"Big Data Firms Collect, Mine and Sell up to 75,000 Individual Data Points on Every Consumer," by Stephanie Simon and Josh Gerstein, Politico, May 14, 2014. Reprinted by permission.

Many people worry about government surveillance in this digital age, but perhaps a bigger worry is the degree to which corporations know your habits, behaviors, and preferences.

The National Security Agency might be tracking your phone calls. But private industry is prying far more deeply into your life.

Commercial data brokers know if you have diabetes. Your electric company can see what time you come home at night. And tracking companies can tell where you go on weekends by snapping photos of your car's license plate and cataloging your movements.

Private companies already collect, mine and sell as many as 75,000 individual data points on each consumer, according to a Senate report. And they're poised to scoop up volumes more, as technology unleashes a huge wave of connected devices—from sneaker insoles to baby onesies to cars and refrigerators—that quietly track, log and analyze our every move.

Congress and the administration have moved to rein in the National Security Agency in the year since Edward Snowden disclosed widespread government spying. But Washington has largely given private-sector data collection a free pass. The result: a widening gap in oversight as private data mining races ahead. Companies are able to scoop up ever more information—and exploit it with ever greater sophistication—yet a POLITICO review has found deep reluctance in D.C. to exercise legislative, regulatory or executive power to curb the big business of corporate cybersnooping.

The inertia—and lack of a serious legislative push—on private-sector data mining has several causes. Many Republicans are averse to any new regulation of business. Many Democrats are skittish about alienating campaign donors in Silicon Valley.

[…]

Polls suggest that Americans want more protections. A national survey by Pew Research last fall found two-thirds of Internet users said current laws weren't adequate to protect consumer privacy online.

[…]

"It's Kind of Creepy"

The technological advances and cheap data storage have created surveillance opportunities that make logging phone calls look downright quaint.

At the mall, the corner store or the casino, hidden cameras may be snapping photos of your face and relaying them to companies that identify you, note your habits and trace your movements.

At home, smart meters can tell whether you have a plasma TV and what time you cook dinner. (Or even, perhaps, whether you're growing marijuana in the basement.)

If you take more conventional prescription drugs, your pill bottles may soon email your doctor to let him know if you've been taking your medication.

Your car may let your mechanic know that your tires need rotating.

Your TV's set-top box may soon be able to sense what you're doing while you're watching a show—snacking? snuggling? mopping?—and broadcast ads appropriate to the situation.

At school, your child's online textbooks may be tracking his every click to understand how his brain works. Some publishers boast that they can tell when a student is on the verge of forgetting, say, how to multiply fractions—and can then send him a lesson custom-tailored to his learning style to fix that skill permanently in his memory.

Rep. Jason Chaffetz (R-Utah), who has fought NSA surveillance and is pushing a bill to limit government use of GPS-type data, seemed surprised when told by POLITICO about how much information on individuals is held in commercial databases.

"It's kind of creepy," he said. "People have a reasonable expectation of privacy from not only their government but from other individuals as well."

In talking up big data, companies tout innovations they say will make the world safer, more convenient and more efficient. Automobile companies, for instance, are developing "connected cars" able to communicate with one another—and with stop signs and traffic lights and even nearby pedestrians—in hopes of making driving far less risky.

From a consumer perspective, the possibilities are almost endless. It could be quite handy to have a refrigerator that notes when the milk is expiring and automatically orders more. Some women might love a bra that senses emotions and texts them when stress levels rise.

By 2020, there could be more than 30 billion wireless devices connected to the Internet worldwide, according to ABI Research.

The trade-off: The more data these gadgets collect, the more intimate details they can expose.

"Are they going to be little snitches in our pockets, or are they going to be under our control and serving us?" asked Jay Stanley, a senior policy analyst with the American Civil Liberties Union.

Privacy advocates fear all this information will find its way to the commercial data brokers who compile and sell profiles packed with details about individuals' health, behavior, interests and preoccupations, including education level, political and religious affiliations, and address, phone numbers and email accounts.

Some data brokers slice and dice consumer profiles into categories such as "Ethnic Second-City Strugglers," "X-tra Needy" and "Fragile Families" for ease of marketing, the Senate Commerce Committee reported last year. One company sold lists of families afflicted by specific illnesses, from AIDS to gonorrhea—and even offered a specialty list of rape victims, until a reporter from The Wall Street Journal inquired about it.

It's information that privacy advocates fear could be used to discriminate against individuals—or to target them with advertising cleverly designed to exploit vulnerabilities.

"We cannot even conceive of the ways our data is collected and then used to manipulate us at our weakest moments," said Danielle Citron, a law professor and privacy scholar at the University of Maryland.

The industry responds that such concerns are overhyped.

Jennifer Glasgow, chief privacy officer for the data broker Acxiom, said the industry provides a valuable service by helping companies target their marketing more precisely. She said her company does not collect sensitive health information and sticks mainly to broad categories: Do you like golf? Do you drive a sports car or a minivan? What's your ballpark income?

"Ferrari doesn't want to bring people into the dealership for a free toaster oven if they're in the $30,000 to $50,000 a year income range," she said.

Acxiom launched a website last fall that lets consumers see their data files. About 250,000 have logged in to look, she said—and only 2 percent have opted to scrub their files from the system. About 20 percent have taken the time to correct the file, which suggests to Glasgow that they like having their information available to marketers.

"If you read a lot of the scare stories about data brokers ... and then look at the site, you'll be pleasantly underwhelmed," Glasgow said. "You're going to say, 'That's pretty accurate. It doesn't scare me that they know about that.'"

EVALUATING THE AUTHOR'S ARGUMENTS:

In this viewpoint authors Stephanie Simon and Josh Gerstein discuss some benefits of having companies collect data on consumers. In addition, several people are quoted about privacy concerns. Does the viewpoint make a stronger case for or against allowing companies to collect data?

Chapter 2

Can Data Mining Improve Society?

The potential for data mining is enormous.

Data Can Improve City Life

"Never before has so much information about people—their characteristics, their location and movements, and their activities—been generated."

William Echikson

In the following viewpoint William Echikson reports on research conducted by Professor Rob Kitchin of Ireland, who studies the ways in which cities collect and use data in an effort to improve urban life. As Kitchin notes, electronic devices and sensors can be placed almost anywhere to collect data. Some cities make this information public for individuals to view, allowing people to develop their own apps using the data. Proper use of this data can lead to healthier and better run cities, Kitchin claims. However, legitimate concerns about privacy and security arise when this significant amount of data is collected. Echikson is a foreign correspondent and founder of E+ Europe.

AS YOU READ, CONSIDER THE FOLLOWING QUESTIONS:

1. What are some places sensors may be used in cities?
2. What are some reasons people might want to view the kind of data collected about their city?
3. Why is privacy a concern with city data collection?

Some experts believe that data collection can be used to make positive changes to urban centers around the world.

With funding from the European Research Council, Professor Rob Kitchin of Ireland's National Institute of Regional and Spatial Analysis is finding out how to leverage Big Data to improve city life.

Modern cities generate a flood of data, and much of it is public. Transport companies know how their trains, buses and cars are travelling. Payment systems monitor the availability of parking spaces. CCTVs provide real-time video links. Environmental sensors track air and water quality.

There's even big data on garbage: networked compactor bins use sensors to monitor waste levels and allow collection routes to be optimised.

The Dublin Dashboard

Two years ago, Rob Kitchin, a professor at the National Institute of Regional and Spatial Analysis at Ireland's Maynooth University launched a novel app, the Dublin Dashboard. This publishes sen-

FAST FACT

Sensors can monitor everything from bus speed to air pollution to the amount of garbage in bins.

sor-readings about the city, providing citizens, public sector workers and companies with real-time information, time-series indicator data and interactive maps about all aspects of Ireland's capital. The data sets are compiled on an ongoing basis by the Irish Central Statistics Office and Eurostat.

Kitchin has built an easy to use interactive website featuring maps, graphs and apps. The data available covers a variety of areas, from transport, housing and planning to the environment, emergency services and health.

With a few clicks, Dubliners can check the tides, temperature, shipping, river levels, oxygen and pollution levels, ambient noise, road traffic, parking spaces—even available bike-shares. Camera feeds yield images. Maps break down city population by topics like gender and density.

"And all the data is open," Kitchin says. "Everybody can go and build their own apps off this, or they can just look at it."

Although the Dublin Dashboard obviously useful—and fun—there is a serious side too, translating into what Kitchin calls new forms of governance.

Cities around the world are demonstrating how it works. Atlanta has a purpose-built dashboard room, where city government meets weekly to assess metrics. Rio de Janeiro built an "urban operations centre" with data streams from 30 government agencies, to try to manage the potential chaos of the World Cup in 2014 and the Olympic Games happening there this year.

Many cities have litter bins with sensors to signal when they're full—meaning the garbage trucks can plot more efficient pick-up routes.

Kitchin's Big Data even helps with policing. Based on perfectly reasonable evidence—neighbourhood crime statistics, social media connections, for example—a person may seem statistically likely to commit a crime. With that information, the police or social workers can be pro-active and offer help or warnings.

The problem, says Kitchin, is that "you don't have evidence that this person has committed a crime ... but you're already treating them as a criminal."

Privacy Challenges

Of course, this information torrent often can turn into a dangerous flood. It can lead managers, distracted by all the data, to focus on the wrong problems—what Kitchin calls "technological solutionism." For instance, he says, with more data "you might be able to better manage homelessness, but you're not going to stop people becoming homeless."

The Big Data flood also poses privacy challenges. In January of this year, Kitchin published a new report on the issue. Entitled "Getting smarter about smart cities: Improving data privacy and data security," it argues that the "haphazard" approach to the development of networked technologies for so-called "smart cities" cannot be allowed to continue without taking proper account of privacy challenges.

"Never before has so much information about people—their characteristics, their location and movements, and their activities—been generated. These data can be put to many good uses, but they also raise a number of issues with respect to data privacy, data protection, and data security," the report says.

But the report also cautions against becoming "overly focused" on the negative concerns and harms lest they stifle innovation. While the concerns relating to smart cities are "significant," we need to remain mindful of their potential benefits in producing "more efficient, productive, sustainable, resilient, transparent, fair and equitable cities."

Kitchin recommends the establishment of advisory boards and governance and ethics committees to oversee such smart city projects. An emergency response team should also be appointed to tackle cybersecurity incidents, where data was hacked or compromised.

"I advocate a much more systematic approach that aims to gain the benefits smart-city technologies offer, whilst minimising the potential risks," he says.

In coming years, Kitchin plans to extend the scope of the Dublin Dashboard project to include other data and information such as maps of social media.

In this viewpoint William Echikson quotes Professor Rob
Kitchin on the benefits and challenges of smart cities.
Kitchin claims that good ethics and oversight can reduce
the privacy and security concerns. How strong is his
argument that the benefits of smart cities outweigh the
problems?

Big Data Can Make a Company More Efficient

World Economic Forum

"In order to have big data to analyze in the first place, companies must invest in the latest technologies."

In the following viewpoint the World Economic Forum considers how businesses use big data. Properly collecting and using data can help a company be more efficient and save money. Companies already use data analysis to plan delivery routes. Data can also be analyzed to predict future growth. In addition, understanding current patterns can help a company know where to expand. Finally, data can help a company design a more efficient system of warehouses and factories. Making the best use of data requires having the right technology. Electronic sensors and identification tags can help track how products move. Then the right people must have access to the data in order to understand and use it. The World Economic Forum's mission is to improve global society through cooperation between public and private groups.

"3 Ways Big Data Can Improve Your Supply Chain," World Economic Forum, May 4, 2015. Reprinted by permission.

AS YOU READ, CONSIDER THE FOLLOWING QUESTIONS:
1. Why is it helpful for a delivery company to know the most efficient route?
2. What is the benefit of forecasting customer demand for products?
3. What are some technology tools that can help track data?

I n our work with supply chain operations across a range of industries, we see three opportunities that offer high potential in the near term. Companies that exploit them can generate significant revenues and profits, as well as reduce costs markedly, lower cash requirements, and boost agility.

Visualizing Delivery Routes

Logistics management challenges all but the most sophisticated specialists in "last-mile delivery." Traditional routing software at advanced delivery companies can show drivers exactly where and how they should drive in order to reduce fuel costs and maximize efficiency. The most flexible systems can plan a truck's route each day on the basis of historical traffic patterns. But many ordinary systems still leave a lot to be desired, producing significant slack in schedules and, in many cases, lacking the ability to dynamically visualize and calibrate routes at the street level.

Now, add the difficulty of aligning the deliveries of two or more business units or companies, each of which manages its own delivery system but must work with the others as one. We frequently find that by using big data and advanced analytical techniques to deal with tough supply-chain problems such as these, companies can identify opportunities for savings equal to 15 to 20 percent of transportation costs. Recent advances in geoanalytical mapping techniques, paired with the availability of large amounts of location data and cheap, fast, cloud-based computing power, allow companies to dynamically analyze millions of data points and model hundreds of potential truck-route scenarios. The result is a compelling visualization of delivery routes—route by route and stop by stop.

Companies can use big data to maximize efficiency, improve service, and lower costs.

Consider the challenges experienced during the premerger planning for the combination of two large consumer-products companies. To better model the merger of the companies' distribution networks, the two companies layered detailed geographic location data onto delivery data in a way that made it possible for them to visualize order density and identify pockets of overlap. The companies learned that they shared similar patterns of demand. Vehicle-routing software also enabled rapid scenario testing of dozens of route iterations and the development of individual routes for each truck. Scenario testing helped the companies discover as much as three hours of unused delivery capacity on typical routes after drivers had covered their assigned miles.

Splitting the fleet between two local depots in one major city would reduce the number of miles in each route and allow trucks to deliver greater volume, lowering the effective cost per case. After the merger, trucks would be able to make the same average number of stops while increasing the average drop size by about 50 percent. The savings from a nationwide combination and rationalization of the two networks were estimated at $40 million, or 16 percent of the total costs of the companies combined. All this would come with no significant investment beyond the initial cost of developing better modeling techniques.

By establishing a common picture of the present and a view of the future, the geoanalysis also delivered less quantifiable benefits: the results built confidence that the estimated savings generated as a result of the merger would reflect reality when the rubber met the road and would also create alignment between the two organizations prior to the often difficult postmerger-integration phase. However, results such as these are only the beginning. New visualization tools, combined with real-time truck monitoring and live traffic feeds from telematics devices, open up even more exciting opportunities, such as dynamic rerouting of trucks to meet real-time changes in demand.

Pinpointing Future Demand

Forecasting demand in a sprawling manufacturing operation can be cumbersome and time consuming. Many managers have to rely on inflexible systems and inaccurate estimates from the sales force to predict the future. And forecasting has grown even more complicated in the current era of greater volatility in demand and increasing complexity in product portfolios.

Now, companies can look at vast quantities of fast-moving data from customers, suppliers, and sensors. They can combine that information with contextual factors such as weather forecasts, competitive behavior, pricing positions, and other external factors to determine which factors have a strong correlation with demand and then quickly adapt to the current reality. Advanced analytical techniques can be used to integrate data from a number of systems that speak different languages—for example, enterprise resource planning, pricing, and competitive-intelligence systems—to allow managers a view of things they couldn't see in the past. Companies can let the forecasting system do the legwork, freeing the sales force to provide the raw intelligence about changes in the business environment.

Companies that have a better understanding of what they are going to sell tomorrow can ship products whenever customers request them and can also keep less stock on hand—two important levers for improving operational performance and reducing costs. Essentially, with better demand forecasting, companies can replace inventory with information and meet customers' demands in a much more agile way. We find that companies that do a better job of predicting future demand can often cut 20 to 30 percent out of inventory, depending on the industry, while increasing the average fill rate by 3 to 7 percentage points. Such results can generate margin improvements of as much as 1 to 2 percentage points.

For example, a global technology manufacturer faced significant supply shortages and poor on-time delivery of critical components as a result of unreliable forecasts. Salespeople were giving overly optimistic forecasts, whose effects rippled through the supply chain as the manufacturer ordered more than was really needed to ensure adequate supply. In addition, the company's suppliers ordered too much from their own component suppliers. As a result, inventories started to increase across the value chain.

To understand the causes of poor forecast performance, the company used advanced tools and techniques to analyze more than 7 million data points, including shipment records, historical forecasting performance, and bill-of-material records. The company also ran simulations comparing forecast accuracy with on-time shipping and inventory requirements to identify the point of diminishing returns for improved accuracy. The underlying pattern of demand proved complex and highly volatile, particularly at the component level. Root cause analysis helped identify the sources of the problem, which included the usual delays and operational breakdowns, as well as more subtle but equally powerful factors such as misaligned incentives and an organization structure with too many silos.

In response, the company redesigned its planning process, dedicating more time to component planning and eliminating bottlenecks from data flows and IT processing. Furthermore, by improving the quality of the data for the component planners, the company was able to reduce the time wasted chasing data and fixing errors. And it developed more sophisticated analytical tools for measuring the accuracy of forecasts.

On the basis of these and other organizational and process improvements, the company expects to improve forecast accuracy by up to 10 percentage points for components and 5 percentage points for systems, resulting in improved availability of parts and on-time delivery to customers. The changes are expected to yield an increase in revenues, while lowering inventory levels, delivering better customer service, and reducing premium freight costs.

Simplifying Distribution Networks

Many manufacturers' distribution networks have evolved over time into dense webs of warehouses, factories, and distribution centers sprawling across huge territories. Over time, many such fixed networks have trouble adapting to the shifting flows of supplies to factories and of finished goods to market. Some networks are also too broad, pushing up distribution costs. The tangled interrelationships among internal and external networks can defy the traditional network-optimization models that supply chain managers have used for years.

But today's big-data-style capabilities can help companies solve much more intricate optimization problems than in the past. Leaders can study more variables and more scenarios than ever before, and they can integrate their analyses with many other interconnected business systems. Companies that use big data and advanced analytics to simplify distribution networks typically produce savings that range from 10 to 20 percent of freight and warehousing costs, in addition to large savings in inventories.

A major European fast-moving-consumer-goods company faced these issues when it attempted to shift from a country-based distribution system to a more efficient network spanning the continent. An explosion in the volume and distribution of data across different systems had outstripped the company's existing capacity, and poor data quality further limited its ability to plan.

The company used advanced analytical tools and techniques to design a new distribution network that addressed these rising complexities. It modeled multiple long-term growth scenarios, simulating production configurations for 30 brands spread across more than ten plants, each with different patterns of demand and material flows. It crunched data on 50,000 to 100,000 delivery points per key country and looked at inventory factors across multiple stages. Planners examined numerous scenarios for delivery, including full truck loads, direct-to-store delivery, and two-tier warehousing, as well as different transport-rate structures that were based on load size and delivery direction.

Unlocking insights from this diverse data will help the company consolidate its warehouses from more than 80 to about 20. As a result, the company expects to reduce operating expenses by as much as 8 percent. As the number of warehouses gets smaller, each remaining warehouse will grow bigger and more efficient. And by pooling customer demand across a smaller network of bigger warehouses, the company can decrease the variability of demand and can, therefore, hold lower levels of inventory: it is volatile demand that causes manufacturers to hold more safety stock.

How to Begin

Operations leaders who want to explore these opportunities should begin with the following steps.

Connect the supply chain from end to end

Many companies lack the ability to track details on materials in the supply chain, manufacturing equipment and process control reliability, and individual items being transported to customers. They fail to identify and proactively respond to problems in ways that increase efficiency and address customers' needs. In order to have big data to analyze in the first place, companies must invest in the latest technologies, including state-of-the-art sensors and radio-frequency identification tags, that can build transparency and connections into the supply chain. At the same time, companies should be careful to invest in areas that add the highest business value.

Reward Data Consistency

Many companies struggle to optimize inventory levels because lot sizes, lead times, product SKUs, and measurement units are entered differently into the various systems across the organization. While big-data systems do not require absolutely perfect data quality and completeness, a solid consistency is necessary. The problem is that in many companies, management doesn't assign a high priority to the collection of consistent data. That can change when leaders make the impact of poor data clear and measure and reward consistent standards.

Build cross-functional data transparency

The supply chain function depends on up-to-date manufacturing data, but the manufacturing function may tightly guard valuable reliability data so that mistakes will be less visible. The data could also help customer service, which might inform customers proactively of delayed orders when, for example, equipment breaks down. Data about production reliability, adherence to schedules, and equipment breakdowns should be visible across functions. To encourage people to be more transparent, management might assemble personnel from different functions to discuss the data they need to do their jobs better.

Invest in the right capabilities

Many operations leaders still don't understand how this new discipline can provide a competitive advantage or how to convert big data into the best strategic actions. Hiring a team of top-shelf data scientists to do analytics for analytics sake is not the answer, however. Companies need to both partner with others and develop their own internal, diverse set of capabilities in order to put big data into a strategic business context. Only then will they be able to focus on the right opportunities and get the maximum value from their investments.

Companies that excel at big data and advanced analytics can unravel forecasting, logistics, distribution, and other problems that have long plagued operations.

Those that do not will miss out on huge efficiency gains. They will forfeit the chance to seize a major source of competitive advantage.

EVALUATING THE AUTHOR'S ARGUMENTS:

In this viewpoint the World Economic Forum suggests that big data can greatly help companies. Data collected on product orders and delivery routes can make for faster deliveries. How does improving a business in this way affect customers?

Data Collection Will Improve Health Care

Carol McDonald

"There is a move toward evidence-based medicine, which involves making use of all clinical data available."

In the following viewpoint Carol McDonald considers the use of big data in health care. She notes that in the United States, health care is expensive and yet ranked poorly. She claims that big data can help improve health care and lower costs. The results of treatments could be tracked and analyzed in more detail than they currently are, however. This information should result in better patient care. Meanwhile, the author notes, fraud might be reduced with better data analysis. This could greatly reduce the cost of medical care. McDonald is a technology expert who works with computer systems in health insurance and other industries.

AS YOU READ, CONSIDER THE FOLLOWING QUESTIONS:

1. How can data analysis help prevent fraud, according to the article?
2. How can machine learning help a doctor understand a patient's symptoms, as described in the article?
3. What is the advantage to having monitors track a patient's vital signs?

"How Big Data is Reducing Costs and Improving Outcomes in Health Care," by Carol McDonald, MapR Technologies, June 7, 2016. Reprinted by permission.

If used to its full potential, big data can significantly improve health care in the United States. This would include lowering costs and making health care more affordable.

Health care costs are driving the demand for big-data driven Healthcare applications. U.S. health care spending has outpaced GDP growth for the past several decades and exceeds spending in any other developed country. Despite being more expensive, according to the Organisation for Economic Co-operation and Development (OECD), the US Health System ranks last among eleven countries on measures of access, equity, quality, efficiency, and healthy lives. Standards and incentives for the digitizing and sharing of healthcare data along with improvements and decreasing costs in storage and parallel processing on commodity hardware, are causing a big data revolution in health care with the goal of better care at lower cost.

Value Based Care

A goal of the Affordable Care Act is to improve health care through the meaningful use of health information technology in order to:

- Improve healthcare quality and coordination so that outcomes are consistent with current professional knowledge
- Reduce healthcare costs, reduce avoidable overuse
- Provide support for reformed payment structures

Health Insurance companies, Medicare and Medicaid are shifting from fee-for-service compensation to value based data driven incentives that reward high quality, cost effective patient care and demonstrate meaningful use of electronic health records.

Health Care Data

Unstructured data forms about 80% of information in the healthcare industry and is growing exponentially. Getting access to this unstructured data—such as output from medical devices, doctor's notes, lab results, imaging reports, medical correspondence, clinical data, and financial data—is an invaluable resource for improving patient care and increasing efficiency.

Examples of healthcare data sources that will benefit from big data and analytics:

- Claims: are the documents providers submit to insurance companies to get paid. A key component of the Health Insurance Portability and Accountability Act (HIPAA) is the establishment of national standards for electronic healthcare transactions in order to improve efficiency by encouraging the widespread use of Electronic Document Interchange (EDI) between healthcare providers and insurance companies. Claim transactions include International Classification of Diseases (ICD) diagnostic codes, medications, dates, provider IDs, the cost.
- Electronic Health/Medical Record data (EHR or EMR): Medicare and Medicaid EHR incentive programs were established to encourage professionals and hospitals to adopt and demonstrate meaningful use of certified EHR technology. EHRs facilitate a comprehensive sharing of data with other providers and

medical applications. EHRs contain the data from the delivery of healthcare which includes diagnosis, treatment, prescriptions, lab tests, and radiology. Health Level Seven International (HL7) provides standards for the exchange, integration, sharing, and retrieval of electronic health record data.

- Pharmaceutical R&D: Clinical Trials Data, Genomic Data.
- Patient behavior and sentiment data.
- Medical Device Data: Patient sensor data from the home or hospital.

Big Data Trends in Healthcare

There is a move toward evidence-based medicine, which involves making use of all clinical data available and factoring that into clinical and advanced analytics. Capturing and bringing all of the information about a patient together gives a more complete view for insight into care coordination and outcomes-based reimbursement, population health management, and patient engagement and outreach.

Reducing Fraud Waste and Abuse with Big Data Analytics

The cost of fraud, waste and abuse in the healthcare industry is a key contributor to spiraling health care costs in the United States, but big data analytics can be a game changer for health care fraud. The Centers for Medicare and Medicaid Services prevented more than $210.7 million in healthcare fraud in one year using predictive analytics. UnitedHealthcare transitioned to a predictive modeling environment based on a Hadoop big data platform, in order to identify inaccurate claims in a systematic, repeatable way and generated a 2200% return on their big data/advanced technology.

The key to identifying fraud is the ability to store and go back in history to analyze large unstructured datasets of historical claims and to use machine-learning algorithms to detect anomalies and patterns.

Healthcare organizations can analyze patient records and billing to detect anomalies such as a hospital's overutilization of services in short time periods, patients receiving healthcare services from different hospitals in different locations simultaneously, or identical prescriptions for the same patient filled in multiple locations.

The Centers for Medicare and Medicaid Services uses predictive analytics to assign risk scores to specific claims and providers, to identify billing patterns, and claim aberrancies difficult to detect by previous methods. Rules-based models flag certain charges automatically. Anomaly models raise suspicion based on factors that seem improbable. Predictive models compare charges against a fraud profile and raise suspicion. Graph models raise suspicion based on the relations of a provider; fraudulent billers are often organized as tight networks.

Predictive Analytics to Improve Outcomes

Initiatives such as meaningful use are accelerating the adoption of Electronic Health Records and the volume and detail of patient information is growing rapidly. Being able to combine and analyze a variety of structured and unstructured data across multiple data sources, aids in the accuracy of diagnosing patient conditions, matching treatments with outcomes, and predicting patients at risk for disease or readmission.

Predictive modeling over data derived from EHRs is being used for early diagnosis and is reducing mortality rates from problems such as congestive heart failure and sepsis. Congestive Heart Failure (CHF) accounts for the most health care spending. The earlier it is diagnosed the better it can be treated avoiding expensive complications, but early manifestations can be easily missed by physicians. A machine learning example from Georgia Tech demonstrated that machine-learning algorithms could look at many more factors in patients' charts than doctors, and by adding additional features there was a substantial increase in the ability of the model to distinguish people who have CHF from people who don't.

Predictive modeling and machine learning on large sample sizes, with more patient data, can uncover nuances and patterns that couldn't be previously uncovered. Optum Labs has collected EHRs of over 30 million patients to create a database for predictive analytics tools that will help doctors make Big Data-informed decisions to improve patients' treatment.

Real-time Monitoring of Patients

Healthcare facilities are looking to provide more proactive care to their patients by constantly monitoring patient vital signs. The data from these various monitors can be analyzed in real time and send alerts to care providers so they know instantly about changes in a patient's condition. Processing real-time events with machine learning algorithms can provide physicians' insights to make lifesaving decisions and allow for effective interventions.

EVALUATING THE AUTHOR'S ARGUMENTS:

Viewpoint author Carol McDonald describes ways that collecting and analyzing data could improve the US health care system. She does not address privacy or security concerns. Do the benefits of using data in health care clearly outweigh any possible concerns?

Big Data Failed to Predict the Flu

"Other sources of digital data—from Twitter feeds to mobile phone GPS—have the potential to be useful tools for studying epidemics."

Adam Kucharski

In the following viewpoint Adam Kucharski considers a health tool called Google Flu Trends. The tool was designed to use big data to predict flu epidemics. After some initial success, Google Flu Trends failed to predict a major epidemic. Later, it overestimated the size of a flu epidemic. Despite this failure, some researchers have hope for using data to predict health trends. It is believed that collecting data on search topics, as well as tracking movement through GPS and Twitter feeds, can help experts study public health and the spread of information. Kucharski is a science writer and mathematician focused on infectious diseases.

AS YOU READ, CONSIDER THE FOLLOWING QUESTIONS:

1. What makes Google a good place to study the search terms people use for health research?
2. How did researchers connect search terms with disease levels, according to the article?
3. Why did Flu Trends fail when one year was different from the previous years?

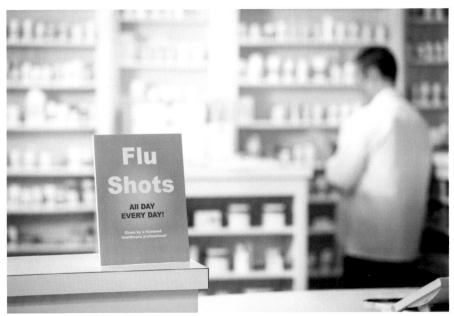

Although it hasn't been entirely successful yet, Google's Flu Trends has the potential to predict flu epidemics.

When people talk about "big data," there is an oft-quoted example: a proposed public health tool called Google Flu Trends. It has become something of a pin-up for the big data movement, but it might not be as effective as many claim.

The idea behind big data is that large amount of information can help us do things which smaller volumes cannot. Google first outlined the Flu Trends approach in a 2008 paper in the journal *Nature*. Rather than relying on disease surveillance used by the US Centers for Disease Control and Prevention (CDC)—such as visits to doctors and lab tests—the authors suggested it would be possible to predict epidemics through Google searches. When suffering from flu, many Americans will search for information related to their condition.

The Google team collected more than 50 million potential search terms—all sorts of phrases, not just the word "flu"—and compared the frequency with which people searched for these words with the amount of reported influenza-like cases between 2003 and 2006. This data revealed that out of the millions of phrases, there were 45 that provided the best fit to the observed data. The team then tested their model against disease reports from the subsequent 2007 epidemic. The predictions appeared to be pretty close to real-life disease levels. Because Flu Trends would able to predict an increase in cases before the CDC, it was trumpeted as the arrival of the big data age.

Prediction Failures

Between 2003 and 2008, flu epidemics in the US had been strongly seasonal, appearing each winter. However, in 2009, the first cases (as reported by the CDC) started in Easter. Flu Trends had already made its predictions when the CDC data was published, but it turned out that the Google model didn't match reality. It had substantially underestimated the size of the initial outbreak.

The problem was that Flu Trends could only measure what people search for; it didn't analyse why they were searching for those words. By removing human input, and letting the raw data do the work, the model had to make its predictions using only search queries from the previous handful of years. Although those 45 terms matched the regular seasonal outbreaks from 2003–8, they didn't reflect the pandemic that appeared in 2009.

Six months after the pandemic started, Google—who now had the benefit of hindsight—updated their model so that it matched the 2009 CDC data. Despite these changes, the updated version of Flu Trends ran into difficulties again last winter, when it overestimated the size of the influenza epidemic in New York State. The incidents in 2009 and 2012 raised the question of how good Flu Trends is at predicting future epidemics, as opposed to merely finding patterns in past data.

In a new analysis, published in the journal PLOS Computational Biology, US researchers report that there are "substantial errors in Google Flu Trends estimates of influenza timing and intensity". This is based on comparison of Google Flu Trends predictions and the actual epidemic data at the national, regional and local level between 2003 and 2013.

Even when search behaviour was correlated with influenza cases, the model sometimes misestimated important public health metrics such as peak outbreak size and cumulative cases. The predictions were particularly wide of the mark in 2009 and 2012.

Valuable Potential

Although they criticised certain aspects of the Flu Trends model, the researchers think that monitoring internet search queries might yet prove valuable, especially if it were linked with other surveillance and prediction methods.

Other researchers have also suggested that other sources of digital data—from Twitter feeds to mobile phone GPS—have the potential to be useful tools for studying epidemics. As well as helping to analyse outbreaks, such methods could allow researchers to analyse human movement and the spread of public health information (or misinformation).

Although much attention has been given to web-based tools, there is another type of big data that is already having a huge impact on disease research. Genome sequencing is enabling researchers to piece together how diseases transmit and where they might come from. Sequence data can even reveal the existence of a new disease variant: earlier this week, researchers announced a new type of dengue fever virus.

There is little doubt that big data will have some important applications over the coming years, whether in medicine or in other fields. But advocates need to be careful about what they use to illustrate the ideas. While there are plenty of successful examples emerging, it is not yet clear that Google Flu Trends is one of them.

EVALUATING THE AUTHOR'S ARGUMENTS:

In this viewpoint Adam Kucharski explains the failures of Google's predictive tools but is quick to emphasize the future potential of such tools. How do you think big data could be used to improve the health of our society?

Big Data Helps Determine Our Leaders

Teradata India

"Obama's data advantage was such that the depth and breadth of the campaign's digital operation reached beyond anything politics had ever seen."

In the following viewpoint Teradata India looks at big data and politics. According to the author, Barack Obama's 2012 reelection campaign was the first to make major use of big data. Prime Minister Modi of India also used big data in his successful campaign. Now several political parties in India design campaigns around the use of data. In an election, data can be used to recruit volunteers and raise funds. It can help politicians target ads to specific groups. Social media can also encourage more people to vote. The author predicts that these examples are only the beginning of using big data in political elections. Teradata India is a corporation that manages large data warehousing operations.

AS YOU READ, CONSIDER THE FOLLOWING QUESTIONS:

1. When did data analysis become an important part of political elections?
2. How does social media allow politicians to reach potential voters?
3. Is the use of data replacing the use of "gut instinct" when designing ad campaigns, according to the article?

"Why Big Data Is The New Game-Changer In Elections," contributed by Teradata India, March 16, 2017. Reprinted by permission.

Politicians are only just beginning to realize the potential that big data can bring to their campaigns.

Barack Obama's campaign in 2012 was arguably the first to adopt big data as a differentiator in the elections. Obama's data advantage was such that the depth and breadth of the campaign's digital operation, from political and demographic data mining to voter sentiment and behavioural analysis, reached beyond anything politics had ever seen.

How They Did It

The Obama campaign management team launched a full-scale integrated campaign, leveraging TV, web, mobile, tele-calling, social media and analytics to directly target potential voters and donors with tailored messages during the lead up to the elections. They hired a multi-disciplinary team of statisticians, predictive modellers, data-mining experts, mathematicians, software programmers and quantitative analysts. One of the key tasks of this team was data consolidation. They worked on bringing together data from many disparate databases to create a single, massive system that merged information collected from pollsters, fundraisers, field workers and consumer databases as well as social-media and mobile contacts with the Democratic voter files. The advantage of having an integrated system is that analytics could be performed effectively across multiple datasets from multiple channels. Furthermore, the information could be shared across the entire organisation seamlessly, without multiple versions of the same data or potential data quality issues. A single version of truth is extremely critical for decision-making in such scenarios. The effective use of big data analytics in the Barack Obama campaign is cited by analysts as one of the major reasons for his victory.

What the Obama campaign did in 2012, Prime Minister Modi did in 2014, though on a smaller scale. With the help of Prashant Kishor, Prime Minister Modi brought a professional touch to his campaign, making heavy use of data analytics and social media to craft messages that appealed to the people. Data analytics helped in refurbishing the engagement campaigns, as well as in creating appropriate strategies to increase voter engagement in key states. Data analytics also helped in recruiting volunteers and raising funds for the election.

The Future of Big Data and Politics

Realising how big data and its resultant analysis can profoundly affect election campaigns and may even go on to determine winners, parties not just limited to the BJP or the Congress but even others such as AAP etc have begun to make use of our digital footprints to design electoral strategies. That said, however, it will be some time before personality profiling—right down to attitudinal factors revealed in consumer and lifestyle habits—can enable targeted ads directed at voters. Even in the build-up to the UP and Punjab elections, for example, touted as critical for the BJP and the Congress both, the ads being run continue to be largely focused on macro issues such as law and order and education. However, a more important aspect in these elections was to get first-time voters to come out to vote and that has been very successful thanks to the aggressive digital engagement strategies by campaign managers across the political parties. Irrespective of who wins or loses, the data from these elections will become important fodder for the next big elections—the 2019 general elections, now just a little over two years away. As the ecosystem matures, expect more customised ads targeting specific groups rather than single ads being targeted at an entire demographic in the run-up to the general elections.

On their part, politicians are increasingly taking the digital route to garner online influence. Prime Minister Modi, for example, has 27.1 million followers on Twitter (up from 8.5 million in 2014) and more than 39 million subscribe to his Facebook page. Younger politicians such as Rahul Gandhi or Akhilesh Yadav have 1.5 million

FAST FACT

Politicians and political parties use data when designing ads asking people to vote a certain way. The data is gathered from polls, consumer records, and social media activity.

and 2.4 million followers respectively. Being a youth leader and no stranger to the power of digital, Akhilesh even tweeted a photograph of him and his wife posing with the directors of Facebook recently. With billions of daily social media interactions, created with each Facebook like and share and a twitter tweet, Indians young and old alike, armed with a plethora of mobile devices, are leaving a huge digital footprint in their wake. Political brand managers are working relentlessly to find new ways to sort through this voluminous data to create, specific and targeted messaging for constituents and voters alike, which are no longer limited to election time. Instead, the idea is to provide them with a seamless user experience at all times, as they move between channels and touch points, whether TV, computer, mobile devices or tablets.

Are there any lessons to draw from the success of big data mining in elections? To begin with, the era of relying on gut instinct (usually predictions made by political experts) is over—a clear demonstration of analytics fuelled by big data and advancement in computing technology has now become an integral part of the campaigning process. But it's not just politics where this is relevant. Whether it's business and finance, the social sectors, government or scientific initiatives, a data-driven approach is more likely to create meaningful impact than a non-data-driven one. And for inspiration, the incredible case studies of how Obama, Modi and Trump won the digital battle will remain fresh for some time to come!

Chapter 3

Does Data Mining Keep Us Safer?

Safety is one justification for surveillance of our data.

Government Surveillance Is a Failure

Rachel Levinson-Waldman

In the following viewpoint Rachel Levinson-Waldman criticizes government surveillance programs. She argues that these programs are an invasion of our privacy. Even worse, she claims, they are not successful. Too much data makes it difficult to find the important information. She quotes several government officials who agree. She then turns to the question of data mining. This process uses computers to analyze large volumes of data. However, the author claims, this has not been successful in identifying terrorists. Levinson-Waldman works for the Brennan Center for Justice at NYU School of Law. This institute's stated goal is to improve democracy and justice.

"Intelligence and law enforcement agencies are increasingly drowning in data; the more that comes in, the harder it is to stay afloat."

AS YOU READ, CONSIDER THE FOLLOWING QUESTIONS:
1. Why is too much data a problem?
2. Why will data mining not help identify terrorists, according to the article?
3. According to the author, what will happen to someone wrongly suspected of terrorism?

"Against Our Values—And Bad at Keeping Us Safe," by Rachel Levinson-Waldman, The New Republic, June 8, 2013. Reprinted by permission.

Data collected by the government is ostensibly for the protection of citizens, but some experts believe it amounts to nothing more than an invasion of privacy.

In the past 48 hours, the American public has been rocked by revelations about the scope of domestic government surveillance. First, we learned that the National Security Agency receives information about the majority of domestic and international phone calls placed in this country. Then we discovered that the NSA and FBI collaborate to vacuum up real-time information from the servers of most major Internet companies as well, including the content of emails, video chats, documents, and more. Although this program is ostensibly directed at gathering data about foreigners, it is likely to sweep in significant amounts of information about Americans too.

There are, needless to say, significant privacy and civil-liberties concerns here. But there's another major problem, too: This kind of dragnet-style data capture simply doesn't keep us safe.

A Flood of Data

First, intelligence and law enforcement agencies are increasingly drowning in data; the more that comes in, the harder it is to stay afloat. Most recently, the failure of the intelligence community to intercept the 2009 "underwear bomber" was blamed in large part on a surfeit of information: according to an official White House review, a significant amount of critical information was "embedded in a large volume of other data." Similarly, the independent investigation of the alleged shootings by U.S. Army Major Nidal Hasan at Fort Hood concluded that the "crushing volume" of information was one of the factors that hampered the FBI's analysis before the attack.

Multiple security officials have echoed this assessment. As one veteran CIA agent told *The Washington Post* in 2010, "The problem is that the system is clogged with information. Most of it isn't of interest, but people are afraid not to put it in." A former Department of Homeland Security official told a Senate subcommittee that there was "a lot of data clogging the system with no value." Even former Defense Secretary Robert Gates acknowledged that "we've built tremendous capability, but do we have more than we need?" And the NSA itself was brought to a grinding halt before 9/11 by the "torrent of data" pouring into the system, leaving the agency "brain-dead" for half a week and "[unable] to process information," as its then-director Gen. Michael Hayden publicly acknowledged.

Data Mining

National security hawks say there's a simple answer to this glut: data mining. The NSA has apparently described its computer systems as having the ability to "manipulate and analyze huge volumes of data at mind-boggling speeds." Could those systems pore through this information trove to come up with unassailable patterns of terrorist activity? The Department of Defense and security experts have concluded that the answer is no: There is simply no known way to effectively anticipate terrorist threats.

Credit card companies are held up as the data-mining paradigm. But the companies' success in detecting fraud is due to factors that don't exist in the counterterrorism context: the massive volume of transactions, the high rate of fraud, the existence of identifiable patterns (for instance, if a thief tests a stolen card at a gas station to check if it works, and then immediately purchases more expensive items), and the relatively low cost of a false positive: a call to the card's owner and, at worst, premature closure of a legitimate account.

By contrast, there have been a relatively small number of attempted or successful terrorist attacks, which means that there are no reliable "signatures" to use for pattern modeling. Even in the highly improbable and undesirable circumstance that the number of attacks rises significantly, they are unlikely to share enough characteristics to create reliable patterns.

Moreover, the surveillance programs that have been disclosed pull in a huge range of data: phone records, emails, Web searches, credit card transactions, documents, live chats. And that's just what we know so far. Not only does this information raise First Amendment concerns where it "accidentally" includes Americans' communications, purchases, and more, but the variety greatly complicates the data-mining process. *The Wall Street Journal* has editorialized that this large sample size is simply a necessary byproduct of the mechanics of data mining, allowing the NSA to "sweep broadly to learn what is normal and refine the deviations." But as the libertarian Cato Institute has argued, not only is such a system "offensive to traditional American freedom," it can be evaded if the terrorists "act as normally as possible."

And when the government gets it wrong—which it will—the consequences are far-reaching. A person falsely suspected of involvement in a terrorist scheme will become the target of long-term scrutiny by law enforcement and intelligence agencies. She may be placed on a watchlist or even a no-fly list, restricting her freedom to travel and ensuring that her movements will be monitored by the government. Her family and friends may become targets as well.

The FBI's and NSA's scheme is an affront to democratic values. Let's also not pretend it's an effective and efficient way of keeping us safe.

EVALUATING THE AUTHOR'S ARGUMENTS:

In this viewpoint, Rachel Levinson-Waldman attacks government surveillance programs. She claims they are an invasion of privacy and not effective. Do her arguments support both of these claims?

Data Mining Won't Stop Terrorism, but It Is One Step Closer to the Police State

American Civil Liberties Union of Massachusetts

"There is no particular risk profile for people who are likely to commit heinous acts of violence. And furthermore, those people intent on doing real harm will go out of their way to study the latest law enforcement approach, and work diligently to get around it."

In the following viewpoint, the American Civil Liberties Union of Massachusetts (ACLUm) assesses the success of data mining companies that are meant to sort and analyze the floods of surveillance data. These companies comb through masses of data to put together neat packages on those with the highest assessed threats. But do they work? The author contends that this is a losing proposition because terrorists cannot be detected through predictive data; one of the success strategies of terrorism is the element of surprise. Even if data mining could stop terrorist acts, the author argues, the high cost of privacy is not worth it. The ACLU is a nonprofit organization that defends the rights and liberties guaranteed under the US Constitution.

"Data-mining: Terrorism Prevention or Social Control?" ACLU.org, December 12, 2011. Reprinted by permission.

1. What is the CIA's "favorite" data analysis company, according to the viewpoint?
2. Does Palantir succeed in preventing terrorism, according to the viewpoint?
3. What crime did Jared Loughner commit?

You may or may not have heard of the CIA's favorite data analysis company, Palantir, which currently operates out of Facebook's old offices in Palo Alto, California. But you likely have heard something about data mining software more generally; it's supposed to be the silver bullet that solves the data-flood problem for the world's spy agencies, which can't seem to know enough about our every movement, thought, purchase, communication, etc.

Software like Palantir is meant to make sense out of the mass of swirling data that clogs databases at the FBI, CIA, DOD, NYPD, LAPD, and increasingly state and local police fusion centers. Those databases contain intimate information about all of us—and yet the vast majority of us aren't plotting violent schemes, but simply going about our quotidian, daily lives. Palantir and like-programs, the story goes, solve the drowning-in-data problem by "connecting the dots," piecing together seemingly unrelated data points to help intelligence and law enforcement agents distinguish between those people who are planning to bomb something, and those who are not.

Palantir does something besides highlight the supposedly dangerous among us, however. As Businessweek reports in a lengthy piece on the company:

> An organization like the CIA or FBI can have thousands of different databases, each with its own quirks: financial records, DNA samples, sound samples, video clips, maps, floor plans, human intelligence reports from all over the world. Gluing all that into a coherent whole can take years. Even if that system comes together, it will struggle to handle different types of data—sales records on a spreadsheet, say, plus video surveillance images. What Palantir (pronounced

Data mining companies are tasked with analyzing the tremendous quantities of data collllected by the US government in an effort to counter terrorism.

Pal-an-TEER) does, says Avivah Litan, an analyst at Gartner (IT), is "make it really easy to mine these big data sets." The company's software pulls off one of the great computer science feats of the era: It combs through all available databases, identifying related pieces of information, and puts everything together in one place.

"Everything together in one place." Sounds creepy, right? It is. And contrary to claims made by Palantir, the CIA and even the Businessweek piece, it doesn't succeed in preventing terrorism. It can't, because data mining and data analysis programs rely on patterns of suspicious behavior in order to determine who is a 'risk'. But as a Homeland Security funded study showed in 2008, predictive terrorism modeling does not work. Why? There is no particular risk profile for people who are likely to commit heinous acts of violence. And furthermore, those people intent on doing real harm will go out

FAST FACT

A 2014 study by the New America Foundation found that the NSA's data mining program had "no discernable impact on preventing acts of terrorism."

of their way to study the latest law enforcement approach, and work diligently to get around it.

We've all heard the basic patterns to look out for: paying cash for one way plane tickets; young men traveling alone; buying large quantities of fertilizer far from a farm, etc. But the 9/11 attacks were so successful precisely because they were so unexpected. What makes the CIA think that the next round of spectacular attacks—if indeed it comes—will be anything like what it has seen before? In other words, how do you model for an infinite number of possible approaches?

You can't. So Palantir won't stop terrorism, full stop. But on the other hand, data-mining software like Palantir is very useful for maintaining social control over people who are not constantly trying to evade the surveillance state, who are simply going about their normal lives under its ever-watchful eye.

The ways in which Palantir can be deployed as a tool for social control are seemingly limitless:

> *Using Palantir technology, the FBI can now instantly compile thorough dossiers on U.S. citizens, tying together surveillance video outside a drugstore with credit-card transactions, cellphone call records, e-mails, airplane travel records, and Web search information.*

If the police want to know what you are doing and where you are going, they can. But towards what end? Can they really discern from your captured images and web reading habits if you are a threat to society? Could Palantir have predicted and therefore stopped Jared Loughner from taking a gun to the shopping mall in Arizona and shooting it up, killing and injuring many? If so, why didn't it?

Even though DHS found in 2008 that data mining used to predict terrorism doesn't work and is too great an assault on personal privacy even if it did, there are even more basic questions we should ask ourselves before we consent to giving up our most basic rights to privacy and personal integrity to the state.

Foremost among these questions is: Can the government keep us safe from all harm at all times? Furthermore, do we want to live in a society wherein we give up all of our privacy, trading our sacred human dignity for (false) promises of personal safety? And if the true aim of the CIA's use of programs like Palantir is public safety, can the government use the technology to prevent car accidents and domestic homicides, which kill tens of thousands more Americans every year than terrorism?

The answers to these questions are obvious. It's time to say 'no' to the culture of fear that promotes the police state ideology.

Democracy has its risks; we either accept them, or we instead accept the rise of the creeping police state. We cannot have both.

EVALUATING THE AUTHOR'S ARGUMENTS:

In this viewpoint, the ACLU places a higher value on privacy and individual liberty than on fighting terrorism, in part because data mining has not been proven to work as a counterterrorism tool. If it *were* successful, would you be willing to relinquish your civil rights in order to be safe from terrorists?

Viewpoint

3

Big Data Can Help Predict Crimes

"Data analysis can provide a probability that a particular house will be broken into on a particular day based on historical records for similar houses in that neighborhood on similar days."

H. V. Jagadish

In the following viewpoint, H. V. Jagadish explores the use of data collection by law enforcement to predict and solve crimes. While the author admits that the use of such data in what is called "predictive policing" cannot with 100 percent certainty tell police officers who will commit any given crime, it can provide them with a lot of pertinent information to aid in the reduction of crime. The author is careful to note that predictive policing, even if it proves to be effective in crime reduction, could be a slippery slope and challenge our civil rights. Jagadish is the Bernard A. Galler collegiate professor of electrical engineering and computer science at the University of Michigan. His area of work is data science.

AS YOU READ, CONSIDER THE FOLLOWING QUESTIONS:

1. What Hollywood movie does the author use to illustrate predictive policing?
2. Rather than certainty, what can data give law enforcement officials?
3. What is the author's example of Tyrone Brown intended to prove?

Local police use collected data to predict, thwart, and solve crimes.

Police departments, like everyone else, would like to be more effective while spending less. Given the tremendous attention to big data in recent years, and the value it has provided in fields ranging from astronomy to medicine, it should be no surprise that police departments are using data analysis to inform deployment of scarce resources. Enter the era of what is called "predictive policing."

Some form of predictive policing is likely now in force in a city near you. Memphis was an early adopter. Cities from Minneapolis to Miami have embraced predictive policing. Time magazine named predictive policing (with particular reference to the city of Santa Cruz) one of the 50 best inventions of 2011. New York City Police Commissioner William Bratton recently said that predictive policing is "the wave of the future."

The term "predictive policing" suggests that the police can anticipate a crime and be there to stop it before it happens and/or apprehend the culprits right away. As the Los Angeles Times points out, it depends on "sophisticated computer analysis of information about previous crimes, to predict where and when crimes will occur."

At a very basic level, it's easy for anyone to read a crime map and identify neighborhoods with higher crime rates. It's also easy to recognize that burglars tend to target businesses at night, when they are unoccupied, and to target homes during the day, when residents are away at work. The challenge is to take a combination of dozens of such factors to determine where crimes are more likely to happen and who is more likely to commit them. Predictive policing algorithms are getting increasingly good at such analysis. Indeed, such was the premise of the movie Minority Report, in which the police can arrest and convict murderers before they commit their crime.

Predicting a crime with certainty is something that science fiction can have a field day with. But as a data scientist, I can assure you that in reality we can come nowhere close to certainty, even with advanced technology. To begin with, predictions can be only as good as the input data, and quite often these input data have errors.

But even with perfect, error-free input data and unbiased processing, ultimately what the algorithms are determining are correlations. Even if we have perfect knowledge of your troubled childhood, your socializing with gang members, your lack of steady employment, your wacko posts on social media and your recent gun purchases, all that the best algorithm can do is to say it is likely, but not certain, that you will commit a violent crime. After all, to believe such predictions as guaranteed is to deny free will.

Feed in Data, Get Out Probabilities

What data can do is give us probabilities, rather than certainty. Good data coupled with good analysis can give us very good estimates of probability. If you sum probabilities over many instances, you can usually get a robust estimate of the total.

For example, data analysis can provide a probability that a particular house will be broken into on a particular day based on historical records for similar houses in that neighborhood on similar days. An insurance company may add this up over all days in a year to decide how much to charge for insuring that house.

A police department may add up these probabilities across all houses in a neighborhood to estimate how likely it is that there will be a burglary in that neighborhood. They can then place more officers in neighborhoods with higher probabilities for crime with the idea that police presence may deter crime. This seems like a win all around: less crime and targeted use of police resources. Indeed the statistics, in terms of reduced crime rates, support our intuitive expectations.

Likely Doesn't Mean Definitely

Similar arguments can be used in multiple arenas where we're faced with limited resources. Realistically, customs agents cannot thoroughly search every passenger and every bag. Tax authorities cannot audit every tax return. So they target the "most likely" culprits. But likelihood is very far from certainty: all the authorities know is that the odds are higher. Undoubtedly many innocent individuals are labeled "likely." If you're innocent but get targeted, it can be a big hassle, or worse.

Incorrectly targeted individuals may be inconvenienced by a customs search, but predictive policing can do real harm. Consider the case of Tyrone Brown, recently reported in The New York Times. He was specifically targeted for attention by the Kansas City police because he was friends with known gang members. In other words, the algorithm picked him out as having a higher likelihood of committing a crime based on the company he kept. They told him he was being watched and would be dealt with severely if he slipped up.

The algorithm didn't "make a mistake" in picking out someone like Tyrone Brown. It may have correctly determined that Tyrone was more likely to commit a murder than you or I. But that is very different from saying that he did (or will) kill someone.

Suppose there's a one-in-a-million chance that a typical citizen will commit a murder, but there is a one-in-a-thousand chance that Tyrone will. That makes him a thousand times as likely to commit a murder as a typical citizen. So it makes sense statistically for the police to focus their attention on him. But don't forget that there is only a one-in-a-thousand chance that he commits a murder. For a thousand such "suspect" Tyrones, there is only one who is a murderer and 999 who are innocent. How much are we willing to inconvenience or harm the 999 to stop the one?

Kansas city is far from being alone in this sort of preemptive contact with citizens identified as "likely to commit crimes." Last year, there was considerable controversy over a similar program in Chicago.

Balancing Crime Reduction with Civil Rights

Such tactics, even if effective in reducing crime, raise civil liberty concerns. Suppose you fit the profile of a bad driver and have accumulated points on your driving record. Consider how you would feel if you had a patrol car follow you every time you got behind the wheel. Even worse, it's likely, even if you're doing your best, that you will make an occasional mistake. For most of us, rolling through a stop sign or driving five miles above the speed limit is usually of little consequence. But since you have a cop following you, you get a ticket for every small offense. In consequence, you end up with an even worse driving record.

Yes, data can help make predictions, and these predictions can help police expend their resources smarter. But we must remember that a probabilistic prediction is not certainty, and explicitly consider the harm to innocent people when we take actions based on probabilities. More broadly speaking, data science can bring us many benefits, but care is required to make sure that it does so in a fair manner.

EVALUATING THE AUTHOR'S ARGUMENTS:

Viewpoint author H. V. Jagadish is careful to balance his argument by discussing the potential pitfalls of using big data for predictive policing. Do you think he thinks predictive policing is a positive thing? How does the author's language support your answer?

Viewpoint

4

Data Mining Can Be Discriminatory

Jeremy Kun

"Carelessly trusting an algorithm allows dominant trends to cause harmful discrimination or at least have distasteful results."

In the following viewpoint Jeremy Kun looks at the issue of "fairness" in algorithms. He describes the potential bias in programs that depend on algorithms. Bias is a prejudice against a person, group, or thing. Sexism and racism are examples of bias. Kun claims that data may contain bias, which then adds a bias to the algorithm using that data. Kun ends by calling on businesses to share their data with researchers. He suggests that this is necessary when trying to understand and evaluate how well algorithms work. Kun is a theoretical computer scientist pursuing a PhD in mathematics.

AS YOU READ, CONSIDER THE FOLLOWING QUESTIONS:

1. The author suggests that police could use an algorithm to excuse their own bias. What does he mean by this?
2. Can an algorithm be biased, according to the author?
3. Why are companies unwilling to share how their algorithms work?

Big data can reveal biases and, in turn, encourage discrimination when applied to social problems.

> *"This program had absolutely nothing to do with race … but multi-variable equations."*

That's what Brett Goldstein, a former policeman for the Chicago Police Department (CPD) and current Urban Science Fellow at the University of Chicago's School for Public Policy, said about a predictive policing algorithm he deployed at the CPD in 2010. His algorithm tells police where to look for criminals based on where people have been arrested previously. It's a "heat map" of Chicago, and the CPD claims it helps them allocate resources more effectively.

Chicago police also recently collaborated with Miles Wernick, a professor of electrical engineering at Illinois Institute of Technology, to algorithmically generate a "heat list" of 400 individuals it claims have the highest chance of committing a violent crime. In response to criticism, Wernick said the algorithm does not use "any racial, neighborhood, or other such information" and that the approach is "unbiased" and "quantitative." By deferring decisions to poorly understood algorithms, industry professionals effectively shed accountability for any negative effects of their code.

But do these algorithms discriminate, treating low-income and black neighborhoods and their inhabitants unfairly? It's the kind of question many researchers are starting to ask as more and more industries use algorithms to make decisions. It's true that an algorithm itself is quantitative—it boils down to a sequence of arithmetic steps for solving a problem. The danger is that these algorithms, which are trained on data produced by people, may reflect the biases in that data, perpetuating structural racism and negative biases about minority groups.

There are a lot of challenges to figuring out whether an algorithm embodies bias. First and foremost, many practitioners and "computer experts" still don't publicly admit that algorithms can easily discriminate. More and more evidence supports that not only is this possible, but it's happening already. The law is unclear on the legality of biased algorithms, and even algorithms researchers don't precisely understand what it means for an algorithm to discriminate.

Being Quantitative Doesn't Protect Against Bias

Both Goldstein and Wernick claim their algorithms are fair by appealing to two things. First, the algorithms aren't explicitly fed protected characteristics such as race or neighborhood as an attribute. Second, they say the algorithms aren't biased because they're "quantitative." Their argument is an appeal to abstraction. Math isn't human, and so the use of math can't be immoral.

Sadly, Goldstein and Wernick are repeating a common misconception about data mining, and mathematics in general, when it's applied to social problems. The entire purpose of data mining is to discover hidden correlations. So if race is disproportionately (but not explicitly) represented in the data fed to a data-mining algorithm, the algorithm can infer race and use race indirectly to make an ultimate decision.

Autocomplete features are generally a tally. Count up all the searches you've seen and display the most common completions of a given partial query. While most algorithms might be neutral on the face, they're designed to find trends in the data they're fed. Carelessly trusting an algorithm allows dominant trends to cause harmful discrimination or at least have distasteful results.

Beyond biased data, such as Google autocompletes, there are other pitfalls, too. Moritz Hardt, a researcher at Google, describes what he calls the sample size disparity. The idea is as follows. If you want to predict, say, whether an individual will click on an ad, most algorithms optimize to reduce error based on the previous activity of users.

But if a small fraction of users consists of a racial minority that tends to behave in a different way from the majority, the algorithm may decide it's better to be *wrong* for all the minority users and lump them in the "error" category in order to be more accurate on the majority. So an algorithm with 85% accuracy on US participants could err on the entire black sub-population and still seem very good.

Hardt continues to say it's hard to determine why data points are erroneously classified. Algorithms rarely come equipped with an explanation for why they behave the way they do, and the easy (and dangerous) course of action is not to ask questions.

Extent of the Problem

While researchers clearly understand the theoretical dangers of algorithmic discrimination, it's difficult to cleanly measure the scope of the issue in practice. No company or public institution is willing to publicize its data and algorithms for fear of being labeled racist or sexist, or maybe worse, having a great algorithm stolen by a competitor.

Even when the Chicago Police Department was hit with a Freedom of Information Act request, they did not release their algorithms or heat list, claiming a credible threat to police officers and the people on the list. This makes it difficult for researchers to identify problems and potentially provide solutions.

Legal Hurdles

Existing discrimination law in the United States isn't helping. At best, it's unclear on how it applies to algorithms; at worst, it's a mess. Solon Barocas, a postdoc at Princeton, and Andrew Selbst, a law clerk for the Third Circuit US Court of Appeals, argued together that US hiring law fails to address claims about discriminatory algorithms in hiring.

The crux of the argument is called the "business necessity" defense, in which the employer argues that a practice that has a discriminatory effect is justified by being directly related to job performance. According to Barocas and Selbst, if a company algorithmically decides whom to hire, and that algorithm is blatantly racist but even mildly successful at predicting job performance, this would count as business necessity—and not as illegal discrimination. In other words, the law seems to *support* using biased algorithms.

> # FAST FACT
> Most algorithms will try to improve accuracy by ignoring outlying data. That means the algorithm will get rid of the most unusual data. This could result in ignoring populations that have unusual behavior.

What Is Fairness?

Maybe an even deeper problem is that nobody has agreed on what it means for an algorithm to be fair in the first place. Algorithms are mathematical objects, and mathematics is far more precise than law. We can't hope to design fair algorithms without the ability to precisely demonstrate fairness mathematically. A good mathematical definition of fairness will model biased decision-making in any setting and for any subgroup, not just hiring bias or gender bias.

And fairness seems to have two conflicting aspects when applied to a population versus an individual. For example, say there's a pool of applicants to fill 10 jobs, and an algorithm decides to hire candidates completely at random. From a population-wide perspective, this is as fair as possible: all races, genders and orientations are equally likely to be selected.

But from an individual level, it's as unfair as possible, because an extremely talented individual is unlikely to be chosen despite their qualifications. On the other hand, hiring based only on qualifications reinforces hiring gaps. Nobody knows if these two concepts are inherently at odds, or whether there is a way to define fairness that reasonably captures both. Cynthia Dwork, a Distinguished Scientist at Microsoft Research, and her colleagues have been studying the relationship between the two, but even Dwork admits they have just scratched the surface.

Get Companies and Researchers on the Same Page

There are immense gaps on all sides of the algorithmic fairness issue. When a panel of experts at this year's Workshop on Fairness, Accountability, and Transparency in Machine Learning was asked what the low-hanging fruit was, they struggled to find an answer. My opinion is that if we want the greatest progress for the least amount of work, then businesses should start sharing their data with researchers. Even with proposed "fair" algorithms starting to appear in the literature, without well-understood benchmarks we can't hope to evaluate them fairly.

EVALUATING THE AUTHOR'S ARGUMENTS:

This viewpoint, like the previous one, mentions predictive policing. How does this piece compare to the previous viewpoint in terms of presenting both sides of the argument? Which author includes more personal opinion?

Anonymity on the Internet

Mary Madden and Lee Rainie

"As long as it's not an illegal activity, a person should not have to worry about being spied on."

In the following viewpoint Mary Madden and Lee Rainie discuss methods of protecting privacy. They note that most Americans have concerns about government and business use of their personal data. However, few people use technology to protect their data, according to a survey. People are more likely to take actions that do not require technology. The article discusses a number of methods of hiding or deleting personal data. It looks at the rates people use these methods, according to a survey. It also reports on the reasons people claimed they valued online privacy. It quotes people both in favor of and opposed to protecting online privacy. Madden is an expert on privacy and technology. Rainie is the director of internet, science, and technology research at the Pew Research Center.

AS YOU READ, CONSIDER THE FOLLOWING QUESTIONS:

1. What methods do people most often use to hide their personal data, according to the survey quoted?
2. What are some of the reasons people think online activity should be anonymous?
3. What are some reasons people think online activity should not be anonymous, according to the article?

"Attempts to Obscure Data Collection and Preserve Anonymity," by Mary Madden and Lee Rainie, Pew Research, May 20, 2015. Reprinted by permission.

Even though Americans want to be safe and secure, online privacy is very important. Some internet users go to great lengths to appear as anonymous as possible.

While most Americans support greater limits on data collection by the government and most express low levels of confidence in the capacity of institutions with which they interact on a daily basis to protect their data, few are taking advanced steps to change their behavior or cloak their activities online. The adoption of certain privacy-enhancing tech tools such as using proxy servers and adding privacy-enhancing browser plug-ins has been low, and respondents have stated a variety of reasons for avoiding these measures.

However, other efforts that entail less technical forms of opting-out of data collection are much more widespread. These include activities such as refusing to provide information that isn't relevant to a transaction and creating personal data "noise" by giving misleading or inaccurate information.

A very small number say they have changed their behavior to avoid being tracked recently, but many were already engaged in more common or less technical privacy-enhancing measures.

At the time of the survey, the vast majority of respondents—91%—had not made any changes to their internet or cellphone use to avoid having their activities tracked or noticed. Only 7% reported that they had made these kinds of changes in "recent months."

At the same time, a much larger group had engaged in an array of everyday obfuscation and privacy-enhancing measures. These activities were not necessarily in direct response to news of government monitoring programs, but rather, represent a broad set of measures that respondents may have engaged in. They include:

- Clearing cookies or browser history: 59% have done this.
- Refusing to provide information about themselves that wasn't relevant to the transaction: 57% have done this.
- Set their browser to disable or turn off cookies: 34% have done this.
- Deleted or edited something they posted in the past: 29% have done this.
- Used a temporary username or email address: 25% have done this.
- Given inaccurate or misleading information about themselves: 24% have done this.
- Decided not to use a website because they asked for their real name: 23% have done this.
- Used a public computer to browse anonymously: 12% have done this.
- Asked someone to remove something that was posted about themselves online: 11% have done this.

There are relatively few demographic variations for these questions, with several notable exceptions. Younger adults under the age of 50 are twice as likely as older adults to say they have given misleading or inaccurate information (30% vs. 16%). This younger group is also somewhat more likely to say they have deleted or edited something they posted in the past (36% vs. 21%) or asked someone to remove something posted online (15% vs. 7%). Women are more likely than men to have requested that online information be removed (16% vs. 6%).

Advanced measures, such as the use of proxy servers and encryption are less common.

This survey included somewhat more expansive questions about advanced privacy-enhancing measures such as the use of proxy servers, virtual private networks and encryption across a variety of communications channels, following up on findings reported earlier this year. However, even with comparatively broader language, just one-in-ten Americans said they had adopted these more sophisticated steps to shield their information:

- 10% of adults say they have encrypted their phone calls, text messages or email.
- 9% say they have used a service that allows them to browse the Web anonymously, such as a proxy server, Tor software, or a virtual personal network.

Awareness of government monitoring programs is associated with some privacy-enhancing behaviors.

When looking at levels of surveillance awareness, engagement in privacy-enhancing activities does not vary in significant ways for most activities with several exceptions. Americans who have heard "a lot" about the programs are more likely than those who have heard just "a little" to:

- Set their browser to disable cookies (48% vs. 33%).
- Give inaccurate or misleading information (36% vs. 23%).

Americans continue to value ability to be anonymous in certain online activities.

Across multiple surveys, a majority of the public has indicated that the ability to be anonymous online is important to them. In the current survey, the majority of adults (55%) said that people should have the ability to use the internet completely anonymously for certain kinds of online activities. Another 16% do not think people should be able to remain anonymous when they are online, and 27% said they "don't know."

Men are more likely than women to think people should be able to engage in certain online activities anonymously (61% vs. 49%), but support for internet anonymity does not vary by age. Education is a predictor, but income is not; adults with at least some college education are significantly more likely than those who have not attended college to believe that people should have the ability to use the internet anonymously (66% vs. 40%).

As a follow-up question, respondents were asked: Could you please tell us briefly why you think that people should or should not have the ability to use the internet completely anonymously? The open-ended responses that followed were varied in both length and substance, but tended to cluster around several recurring threads that are examined below.

Why people support the idea of anonymity for some online activities.

A large share of respondents who support anonymity referred to key phrases associated with privacy that were similar to those discussed in the first report from this series. In their explanation of why anonymity was important to preserve, they noted that people have a "right to privacy" or it's "no one's business" what they do online.

Another substantial share cited the idea that as long as a person's online activity does not present a threat to others, that they should have the ability to use the internet completely anonymously for certain kinds of online activities:

Could you please tell us briefly why you think that people should have the ability to use the internet completely anonymously?

> "As long as it's not an illegal activity, a person should not have to worry about being spied on."
> "There are activities which are not considered socially

*acceptable in certain circumstances, which create no harm
to other people."*

*"As long as no criminal activity is involved, why should
anyone's browsing history be tracked if they don't want it
tracked?"*

*"There is a basic right to privacy as long as the activity
does not endanger others. The trick is to distinguish the
activities."*

A range of responses also noted that anonymity is essential to
ensure freedom of expression and that certain activities are compromised without the ability to remain anonymous online.

"Anonymity is the first line of protection for free speech."

*"I think that the internet needs to remain free and
anonymous for it to be a place where people can exchange
ideas and information without fear. If your digital life
can be monitored and saved then you are at the mercy of
whoever ends up with enough money and power to use that
information."*

*"People like to research different things. Just because I
may look up a topic doesn't mean I am a terrorist."*

*"For example, you search for information regarding
a medical condition. Within minutes, you are being
bombarding with advertising for drugs. Now there are
multiple companies that know you are interested in a
particular medical condition and they assume you have it. I
think you should have the privacy to not have everything you
search dumped into an advertising targeting system."*

At the same time, another category of responses presented exceptions to the general idea that people should be able to use the internet
anonymously for certain activities:

*"I think the ability to track an individual's activity online
(but also on phones, etc) creates a real dilemma in the U.S.
—we value our freedom and don't want 'the government'
telling us what to do – and what not to do (e.g. Russia,*

the Middle East) BUT –having lived through 9/11 terrorism…we understand the value of monitoring activity(…).

"Freedom is what this country is based on it should be included in what a person looks at on the computer (except for things like child porn because that is not victimless)."

"Some uses are acceptable, not all. (…) Reading news/magazines online is no different than buying the item on the news stand."

"I think certain kinds of harmless activities should be anonymous, but illegal or grey area activities should be tracked."

Why some people oppose the idea of online anonymity.

The vast majority of responses in opposition to the idea that people should have anonymity for certain online activities noted either the idea that those who are doing no wrong should "have nothing to hide" or argued that anonymity enables a variety of illegal or objectionable activity. Among the specific concerns noted were: child predators, terrorists, human traffickers and cyberbullies. Others noted a range of concerns and the fact that if and when bad things happen, that the offenders should be able to be identified:

Could you please tell us briefly why you think that people should not have the ability to use the internet completely anonymously?

"There are a lot of crazy people that go on line and do bad things, these people should be able to be found, if they need *to be anonymous then maybe they have something to hide."*

"Too much potential for crime. Using the internet anonymously removes responsibility."

"I guess if there was some sort of illegal or threatening activity involved, I'd want that activity monitored, or the ability to trace it back to the originating person/place."

"If you are doing something anonymously then you are probably doing something you shouldn't be doing at all."

Even as they expect anonymity for certain activities online, most assume that motivated people and organizations could uncover details that they wish to keep private.

When respondents were asked to consider how difficult it would be for a motivated person or organization to learn details about their past that they would prefer to keep private, 64% said it would be "not too" or "not at all" difficult for them to uncover that sensitive information. Just 20% felt it would be "very" or "somewhat" difficult.

Men and women report similar responses, but those ages 50 and older (76%) are significantly more likely to believe it would be "not too" or "not at all difficult" when compared with those under the age of 50 (54%). Similarly, those with a college degree are more likely than those who have not attended college to feel more exposed (70% vs. 58%).

EVALUATING THE AUTHOR'S ARGUMENTS:

This viewpoint primarily reports the results of a survey of Americans. The survey looked at opinions on online privacy and what people do to protect their privacy online. Does the article seem to support a specific viewpoint on the issues?

Facts About Data Mining

Editor's note: These facts can be used in reports to add credibility when making important points or claims.

The Age of Data

- Computers were developed in the 1940s. They became widely available in the 1970s. This allowed for greater storage of large amounts of data.
- The Internet was invented in 1969 and became widely used in the 1990s. It allowed data to be shared online quickly and easily. By 1997, the term "big data" was used to describe extremely large sets of data.
- After the year 2000, the amount of digital data available increased dramatically. At the same time, companies developed better methods of handling all this information. Software programs gave companies and organizations the ability to analyze large sets of data.
- In June 2013, Edward Snowden, a former CIA systems analyst, released secret government papers. They revealed how the US National Security Agency (NSA) was spying on US citizens. This opened a debate on what privacy rights citizens have when it comes to government surveillance.
- In March 2015, several US senators drafted a bill called the Data Broker Accountability and Transparency Act. This act would provide guidelines for regulating the data broker industry. At the time of this writing, the act is still under consideration.

Pros and Cons of Data Mining

Pros:

- Businesses can detect errors and fraud quickly.
- Businesses can understand and respond to customer needs and preferences.
- Businesses can improve customer service.

- Health care organizations can improve care.
- The government can identify potential terrorists.
- Cities can improve city services.

Cons:
- Businesses often struggle to understand and properly use data.
- Customers lose privacy when information about them is shared and sold.
- Thieves and hackers may steal data and use it for identity theft or fraud.
- People could be wrongly identified as criminals or potential terrorists.
- Misuse of data can lead to discrimination.

Public Opinion on Data and Privacy

- The Pew Research Center conducted a survey of 498 adults in 2014. It found that Americans place a high value on privacy.
- Sixty-five percent felt that controlling what information is collected about them is very important. Twenty-five percent say this is somewhat important. Social Security numbers were identified as the most sensitive pieces of information. Purchasing habits were considered least sensitive.
- Seventy-four percent of respondents felt it was very important to control *who* can get information about them. Nineteen percent felt that was somewhat important.
- Only 9 percent of survey respondents felt they had a lot of control over information that is collected about them in daily life. Thirty-eight percent said they had some control, 37 percent said they did not have much control, and 13 percent said they had no control at all.
- Fifty-five percent thought they should be able to use the internet anonymously.
- Only 9 percent of respondents had recently changed their internet or cell phone used to avoid having their activities tracked. Fifty-seven percent refused to provide personal information that wasn't relevant to the transaction.

Organizations to Contact

The editors have compiled the following list of organizations concerned with the issues debated in this book. The descriptions are derived from materials provided by the organizations. All have publications or information available for interested readers. The list was compiled on the date of publication of the present volume; the information provided here may change. Be aware that many organizations take several weeks or longer to respond to inquiries, so allow as much time as possible for the receipt of requested materials.

American Civil Liberties Union (ACLU)
125 Broad St., 18th Floor, New York, NY 10004
(212) 549-2500
email: aclu@aclu.org
website: www.aclu.org
The ACLU is a national organization that works to defend Americans' civil rights. It provides legal defense, research, and education. In terms of privacy and technology, the ACLU works to expand the right to privacy and increase the control individuals have over their personal information.

Center for Democracy and Technology (CDT)
1634 I Street NW #1100 , Washington, DC 20006
(202) 637-9800
contact: cdt.org/contact
website: cdt.org
The CDT is a nonprofit organization that champions human rights and civil liberties. In terms of data and privacy, the CDT works to maintain an internet controlled by users. A blog and "insights" section provide news updates and opinion pieces.

Electronic Frontier Foundation (EFF)
815 Eddy Street, San Francisco, CA 94109 USA
(415) 436-9333 x100
email: info@eff.org website: www.eff.org
The Electronic Frontier Foundation (EFF) is a nonprofit organization that works to protect civil liberties in the digital world. The group champions user privacy and free expression along with innovation and technology. The website offers overviews on issues such as internet free speech, privacy, and security, along with updates on news and legal cases.

Electronic Privacy Information Center (EPIC)
1718 Connecticut Avenue, NW, Suite 200, Washington, DC 20009
(202) 483-1140
email: info.epic.org
website: www.epic.org
The Electronic Privacy Information Center (EPIC) is an independent nonprofit research center. Its mission is to protect privacy, freedom of expression, and democratic values in the information age. The group aims to give the public a voice in making decisions about the future of the internet. Sections of EPIC's website cover news, important topics, and resources.

Future of Privacy Forum
1400 Eye Street NW, Suite 450, Washington, DC 20005
(202) 642-9142
contact: fpf.org/contact-us
website: www.fpf.org
The Future of Privacy Forum is a nonprofit organization made up of members from industry, academia, and other leaders. The group supports the ethical use of data. The forum's website includes several resources and pages that cover issues, news, and opinions.

Privacy Research Group

New York University School of Law, 40 Washington Square South
New York, NY 10012.
(212) 998-6013
email: nicole.arzt@nyu.edu
website: www.law.nyu.edu/centers/ili/privacy_research_group
This group is a weekly meeting of students, professors, and industry professionals concerned with privacy in the digital age. Meeting topics cover everything from understanding privacy to debating legal trials over surveillance.

Public Knowledge

1818 N Street, NW, Suite 410, Washington, DC 20036
(202) 861-0020
email: pk@publicknowledge.org
website: www.publicknowledge.org
Public Knowledge promotes freedom of expression and an open internet. The group is concerned with many issues relating to the internet, including online privacy and security.

TechFreedom

110 Maryland Avenue NE, Washington, DC 20002
(202) 803-2867
email: media@techfreedom.org
website: techfreedom.org
Tech Freedom promotes the progress of technology that improves the human condition. It focuses on educating the public, policymakers, and leaders on policies that encourage technology. Issues of interest include privacy, internet free speech, and online security.

For Further Reading

Books

Angwin, Julia. *Dragnet Nation: A Quest for Privacy, Security, and Freedom in a World of Relentless Surveillance*. New York, NY: Times Books, 2014. The author of this book digs deep for an exploration of how the government, private companies, and criminals use and abuse personal data.

Eboch, M. M. *Big Data and Privacy Rights* (Essential Library of the Information Age). Edina, MN: ABDO Essential Library, 2016. This book offers an introductory look at the issues surrounding big data and privacy rights, including how companies, governments, and individuals collect and use data.

Foreman, John W. *Data Smart: Using Data Science to Transform Information into Insight*. Hoboken, NJ: Wiley, 2013. A data scientist explains how to turn data into insights in this book. Digital readers can use a spreadsheet to try each technique themselves.

Greenwald, Glenn. *No Place to Hide: Edward Snowden, the NSA, and the U.S. Surveillance State*. New York, NY: Metropolitan Books, 2014. This fascinating book provides a detailed look at the case of Edward Snowden, who released secret documents showing NSA data collection. Greenwald then turns from his mysterious subject to explore what government surveillance means to the privacy of citizens.

Mitnick, Kevin. *The Art of Invisibility: The World's Most Famous Hacker Teaches You How to Be Safe in the Age of Big Brother and Big Data*. New York, NY: Little, Brown and Company, 2017. This book presents true stories to show how online information is being exploited and offers guidance in staying anonymous.

Payton, Theresa, and Ted Claypoole. *Privacy in the Age of Big Data: Recognizing Threats, Defending Your Rights, and Protecting Your Family*. Lanham, MD: Rowman & Littlefield Publishers, 2014. An introduction to the many ways we are being watched through our digital devices. The authors include advice on tools and behavior changes to increase privacy.

Schneier, Bruce. *Data and Goliath: The Hidden Battles to Collect Your Data and Control Your World.* New York, NY: W. W. Norton & Company, 2015. This book is an overview of privacy and security issues, written by a security expert.

Siegel, Eric. *Predictive Analytics: The Power to Predict Who Will Click, Buy, Lie, or Die.* Hoboken, NJ: Wiley, 2016. An exploration of how data analysis can be used to make predictions. The book includes case studies and techniques.

Periodicals and Internet Sources

Betancourt, Leah, "How Companies Are Using Your Social Media Data," Mashable, March 2, 2010. http://mashable.com/2010/03/02/data-mining-social-media/#VcXkG_BwREqY.

"Big Data and the Future of Privacy," EPIC, October 10 2015. epic.org/privacy/big-data.

Butler, Declan, "When Google Got Flu Wrong," Nature.com, February 13, 2013. http://www.nature.com/news/when-google-got-flu-wrong-1.12413.

Cate, Fred H., and Viktor Mayer-Schönberger, "Notice and Consent in a World of Big Data," *Oxford Journals*, 2013. http://idpl.oxfordjournals.org/content/3/2/67.abstract.

Criddle, Linda, "Online Quizzes and Surveys, and the Real Risks These Represent," I Look Both Ways, November 5, 2015.

Duhigg, Charles, "How Companies Learn Your Secrets," *New York Times Magazine*, February 16, 2012.

Eligon, John, and Timothy Williams, "Police Program Aims to Pinpoint Those Most Likely to Commit Crimes," *New York Times*, September 24, 2015.

Farr, Christina, "Weighing Privacy Vs. Rewards Of Letting Insurers Track Your Fitness," NPR.org, April 9, 2015. http://www.npr.org/sections/alltechconsidered/2015/04/09/398416513/weighing-privacy-vs-rewards-of-letting-insurers-track-your-fitness.

Fortado, Lindsay, Robbin Wigglesworth, and Kara Scannell, "Hedge Funds See a Gold Rush in Data Mining," *Financial Times*, August 28, 2017. https://www.ft.com/content/d86ad460-8802-11e7-bf50-e1c239b45787.

"The Game-changing Benefits of Social Media Data," November 4, 2014. www.promptcloud.com/blog/the-game-changing-benefits-of-social-media-data.

Gorski, Ashley, "Court Chooses to Ignore Overwhelming Evidence of NSA's Mass Internet Spying," ACLU, October 24, 2015. www.aclu.org/blog/speak-freely/court-chooses-ignore-overwhelming-evidence-nsas-mass-internet-spying.

Hardekopf, Bill, "The Big Data Breaches of 2014," *Forbes,* January 13, 2015.

Harvard Business Review Staff. "With Big Data Comes Big Responsibility," *Harvard Business Review,* November 2014.

Hvistendahl, Mara, "Can 'Predictive Policing' Prevent Crime Before It Happens?" *Science*, September 28, 2016. http://www.sciencemag.org/news/2016/09/can-predictive-policing-prevent-crime-it-happens.

Madden, Mary, and Lee Rainie, "Americans' Views About Data Collection and Security," Pew Research Center. May 20, 2015. www.pewinternet.org/2015/05/20/americans-views-about-data-collection-and-security.

McAfee, Andrew, and Erik Brynjolfsson, "Big Data: The Management Revolution," *Harvard Business Review*, October 2012. https://hbr.org/2012/10/big-data-the-management-revolution.

More, Timothy, Theodore "Theo" Forbath, and Allison Schoop, "Customer Data: Designing for Transparency and Trust," *Harvard Business Review*. May 2015. https://hbr.org/2015/05/customer-data-designing-for-transparency-and-trust.

O'Shea, Kellie A., "Use of Social Media in Employment: Should I Fire? Should I Hire?" *Cornell HR Review*, October 30, 2012. http://www.cornellhrreview.org/use-of-social-media-in-employment-should-i-fire-should-i-hire.

Podesta , John, "Big Data and Privacy: 1 Year Out," White House, February 5, 2015. obamawhitehouse.archives.gov/blog/2015/02/05/big-data-and-privacy-1-year-out.

President's Council of Advisors on Science and Technology. "Report to the President: Big Data and Privacy: A Technological Perspective."

The White House, May 2014. www.whitehouse.gov/sites/default/files/microsites/ostp/PCAST/pcast_big_data_and_privacy_-_may_2014.pdf.

Press, Gil, "A Very Short History Of Big Data," *Forbes*, May 9, 2013.

Ross, Jeanne W., Cynthia M. Beath, and Anne Quaadgras, "You May Not Need Big Data After All," *Harvard Business Review*, December 2013. https://hbr.org/2013/12/you-may-not-need-big-data-after-all.

Rushe, Dominic, "Tim Cook challenges Obama with impassioned stand on privacy," *Guardian*, February 13, 2015.

Saltzman, Marc, "How to Browse the Web Anonymously," *USA TODAY*. June 22, 2014.

Tene, Omer, and Jules Polonetsky, "Big Data for All: Privacy and User Control in the Age of Analytics," *Northwestern Journal of Technology and Intellectual Property* Volume 11, Issue 5, Article 1, 2013.

Wikert, Joe, "Here's How Search Will Evolve and Become More Powerful," October 19, 2015. http://jwikert.typepad.com/the_average_joe/2015/10/heres-how-search-will-evolve-and-become-more-powerful.html.

Wren, Kathy, "Big Data and Human Rights, a New and Sometimes Awkward Relationship," AAAS Science and Human Rights Coalition. January 28, 2015. www.aaas.org/news/big-data-and-human-rights-new-and-sometimes-awkward-relationship.

"You Are Being Tracked." ACLU, October 15, 2015. www.aclu.org/feature/you-are-being-tracked.

Websites

Center for Democracy and Technology (www.cdt.org)
The Center for Democracy and Technology is a nonprofit organization that works to maintain an internet controlled by users. The CDT is dedicated to keeping the internet open, innovative, and free. The organization's website includes many news updates, opinion pieces, and other resources.

Electronic Privacy Information Center (www.epic.org)
The Electronic Privacy Information Center works to protect privacy, freedom of expression, and a public voice in decisions about the fu-

ture of the internet. This research center's website cover news, policy issues, and provides information on related resources.

Future of Privacy Forum (www.fpf.org)
The Future of Privacy Forum is a think tank that works to advance responsible data practices. Its website offers news, opinions, information on related events, and other resources.

Stay Safe Online: National Cyber Security Alliance (www.stay-safeonline.org)
The National Cyber Security Alliance provides outreach and education about cybersecurity. This special section targeted to teens and young adults lists books, videos, resources, quizzes, and information on topics such as mobile privacy and social networking.

Index

government surveillance
  and correcting citizen behavior,
    26, 30
  and terrorism prevention, 8,
    78, 80–82, 83–87

H
health care, how data mining can
  improve, 62–67

I
India, use of big data in political
  campaigns, 74, 75
influenza outbreak of 2009, 68–
  71
Instagram, 32
Ireland, use of big data to improve city life, 49–51

J
Jagadish, H. V., 88–92

K
Kitchin, Rob, 48–52
Kucharski, Adam, 68–71
Kun, Jeremy, 93–98

L
Levinson-Waldman, Rachel, 78,
  80–82
Loughner, Jared, 84, 86

M
Madden, Mary, 99–106
McDonald, Carol, 62–67
medical fraud, big data's role in
  reducing, 62, 65–66
Microsoft, 8, 98

Modi, Narendra Damodardas,
  use of data analytics in prime
  minster campaign, 74, 75
Morse v. Frederick, 34
MySpace, 34

N
National Coalition Against Censorship, 31–40

O
Obama, Barack, presidential
  campaign of 2012, 72–74, 75
opting out, of data sharing, 18–
  19

P
Palantir, 84–87
personal data, how it can be protected or deleted, 18–19, 99–
  108
political campaigns, how they
  use data mining, 72–76
predictive policing, 88–92, 93–
  98
proxy servers, 100, 102

R
racism, 12, 93, 95, 96, 97
Rainie, Lee, 99–106

S
sample size disparity, 96
sexism, 93, 96
Shine the Light law, 14
Simcoe, Tim, 21–25
Simon, Stephanie, 41–46
smart cities, 49–51

SnapChat, 32, 36
Snowden, Edward, 43

T
Teradata India, 72–76
Tinker v. Des Moines Independent Community School District, 32
Twitter, 30, 34, 36, 37, 40, 68, 71, 75

U
urban life, how data mining can improve, 48–52
US National Security Agency (NSA), 8, 12, 40, 42, 43, 80–82

W
Wernick, Miles, 94, 95
whistleblowers, 34
World Economic Forum, 53–54, 56–61

Y
Yahoo, 8

Picture Credits